Advance Praise for *Nightingale*

"This powerful memoir tells the story of a young girl whose beloved grandmother provided security in the midst of an otherwise unpredictable and sometimes violent family. Many children in such circumstances would lose hope, but the author transformed her anxiety into passion for making the world a safer place for children and vulnerable adults. The book also provides a rich source of information for those interested in the history of notable Minnesota families. The writing is compelling, and the story is worth reading and taking to heart."

—Harold D. Grotevant, Ph.D.
Rudd Family Foundation Chair and Professor of Psychology,
University of Massachusetts Amherst

Nightingale

Nightingale

A MEMOIR OF MURDER, MADNESS, AND THE MESSENGER OF SPRING

Suzanne Congdon LeRoy

KITAI PRESS · BLOOMINGTON
2013

KITAI PRESS
Post Office Box 385395, Bloomington, MN 55438

First published in the United States by Kitai Press

Nightingale: A Memoir of Murder, Madness, and the Messenger of Spring
Suzanne Congdon LeRoy

ISBN: 978-0-9897489-1-9

Cover photo: Elisabeth Congdon, 1912,
Lake Waban, Wellesley, MA

Printed in the United States of America

For my grandmother, Elisabeth Mannering Congdon

Remember me when I am gone away,
Gone far away into the silent land;
When you can no more hold me by the hand,
Nor I half turn to go yet turning stay...

—Christina Rossetti

PART I

FLEDGLING

ESTATE OF WONDER

The world is full of magic things…
— W.B. Yeats

I am four years old, cozy in a pink flannel nightgown with tiny white lace at the neck. Grandma's soft hand is holding mine.

"I slept here when I was growing up," Grandma says.

Roses are everywhere. Pink roses on the quilt, pink rose bouquets on the wallpaper, tiny pink roses on the lampshade above the headboard, and hand-painted pink roses on the satinwood furniture from Sri Lanka, a place that Grandma says is far, far away. The pink roses on the rug beneath my feet are as soft as velvet.

A tiny crystal chandelier hangs from the archway in the middle of the bedroom. It glows like the moon. The lights on the walls are like candles, and beneath them are pictures of ladies with fancy hairstyles and pretty dresses in a circle of pink.

"Cameos," Grandma tells me.

I trace the painted roses on the chair in front of the desk. There's another chair just like it in front of the dressing table by the bed. Crisp white sheets and a fluffy pink blanket are neatly turned down. The rose quilt, made by Great-grandmother Clara, is carefully folded. The tiny stitches are perfect. I climb into the single bed next to the beautiful wall garden. The pink roses on the wallpaper look so real that I touch the tiny petals. A small pillow in its pressed white case is soft beneath my head.

Grandma leans over, kisses my cheek, and tucks me in. Her soft skin smells pretty, like baby powder.

The pearls of her necklace are smooth between my fingers. Thirteen gold charms jingle on her bracelet as I search for my own charm among the circle of grandchildren. Grandma picks one, points to the writing, and says, "Suzanne." I trace the little girl's face and hair. Grandma calls it a silhouette. On the back of the charm, I find the numbers that tell my birthday: 11-1-1954.

"The house story," I whisper.

"All right," Grandma says. She sits on the edge of the bed and leans toward me. Her eyes twinkle. "This house has a special name."

"Glensheen," I say.

"For the woods, the shiny water, and the pretty valley," Grandma says.

"And the village," I say.

"Yes, the village called Sheen. Far across the ocean in Surrey, England, where the Congdon family lived."

"Long ago."

Grandma nods. "Many men built this house. With brick and stucco."

"Like cement."

"And many types of wood and marble from all over the world," Grandma says.

"And pictures."

"Yes, beautiful art."

"And lots of rooms."

"Thirty-nine," Grandma says.

"And a boathouse," I say.

"And a carriage house."

"For the horses and cows."

"And four greenhouses," Grandma says.

"And a tennis court."

"Can you remember what else?"

"Ummm...the grass for bowling."

"That's right. Lawn bowling," Grandma says. "My father built this house for our family. The Congdon family."

"I know their names," I say. "Great-grandfather Chester, Great-grandmother Clara, Walter, Ned, Marjorie, Helen, Elisabeth—that's *you*, Grandma—and Robert."

"Yes, that's right," she says.

"Baby John didn't live here."

Grandma strokes my cheek with the back of her hand. "No, he died before he was two years old from scarlet fever."

"But Alfred came."

"Yes, he was my cousin."

"He's a Bannister."

"Like my mother Clara."

"Strong men built the house," I say. "Between the creeks."

"Tischer Creek and Bent Brook," Grandma says.

"You watched the ships go by."

"On Lake Superior," she says.

"A big lake."

"The Ojibwe Indians called it Gitchigami."

"Gitchigami," I say, loving the name.

"Gitchigami," Grandma says again.

I wrap my hands around her neck, and I touch her soft hair. The tip of my finger fits in one of the tiny gray curls. "I love you Grandma," I say. I kiss the pink color in her cheek.

"And I love you. Sleep well." She turns off the light above my head. I can still see the pink petals on the wall by the soft light of the hallway. It's so quiet here. Not like at home in Minneapolis. Dad yelling at Mom: *Stop spending so much money!*

And Mom yelling back: *Don't tell me what to do, it's my money!* When they are cross with each other I am afraid. My bedroom at home is at the top of the stairs. Every night I hear Mom and Dad yelling in the living room.

Steve is six and Pete is five. They don't hear the noise. They sleep on the third floor where the bedroom windows are as high as the treetops. The linen closet has labels with my brothers' names on the shelves so the neatly folded sheets and pillowcases are in perfect order. Andy is three and Becky is two. They sleep on the second floor, around the corner from my room. Mom is going to have another baby soon.

But I'm safe here. Grandma is right across the hall.

In the sparkling white bathroom next to the pink room, there's a round white button like a pearl above the giant bathtub. I want to touch it, smooth and shiny, but I can't reach.

Grandma and her gray French poodle are close by in the hallway. "Come Philíppe," Grandma says. The metal tags on his collar jingle.

"Grandma," I say. "A doorbell...in the bathroom."

"Let's go see," she says.

I point to the button on the wall.

Grandma leans over to take a look. "It's a call button," she says. "Long ago we let the maids know that we needed help with the buttons and hooks on our dresses."

"Because they were so fancy?"

"Yes," Grandma says. "That's right. We also let the cook and maids know that we were ready for breakfast."

"Breakfast in the bathroom?" I ask.

"No. It worked a little differently," Grandma says. "I want to show you something."

We head toward the back stairs, past the linen closet with the doors of glass, past the tiny bedrooms for the cook and maids.

Philippe's toenails click on the wood stairs as he runs ahead to the staff dining room.

The oak table and chairs with the carved birds and flowers came from the house Grandma lived in before Glensheen. Grandma says the cook and maids eat the same food as the family, but one hour earlier; that way they aren't hungry when they serve.

Philippe races into the white kitchen that takes up the entire end of the house. He stops and sniffs the air and then he goes into the little pantry with the rolling pins and jars of chocolate chip cookies. There's a sweet smell of chopped apples and cinnamon. The glass pie plate is filled with a pancake made of dough.

The wood door to the basement is partway open. Anna, the German cook, sounds like she is tap dancing down the stairs to the cellar where the apples stay cold. The crates have pictures of the apples and pears that grow on trees in Great-grandfather's orchards in Washington. Grandma and I stayed in the big stone house.

The kitchen walls are covered with lots of sparkly white tiles. Grandma points up high on the wall next to the butler's pantry. Black letters and brass arrows are covered by glass.

"Annunciator," she says. "The arrow points to the person's name when the call button is pressed."

"Oooh, magic," I say.

"Usually ladies ate breakfast in bed because it took them longer to get dressed."

Last time I was at Glensheen, the maids set up a little bed on the pink carpet between Grandma's bed and the fireplace. The gray, pink, and green tiles sparkled when Ole, Grandma's helper, made a fire. The table with the glass top and Grandma's treasures was close by. She let me hold the old coin with the big name. Byzantine.

"We ate breakfast in bed," I say.

"Yes," Grandma says. "We did."

"The white tray had little legs...a pink rose...scrambled eggs and toast and jam...and orange juice!" I say. I hold my hands out wide. "The glass was this big."

"I had the same, with coffee," Grandma says. A tiny yellow-and-white china bowl held the saccharin tablets and the doll-size silver spoon.

"I have something else to show you," Grandma says.

We walk past the blackboard where Grandma writes the daily menus with white chalk, just like she's teaching school. The china cups and plates are stacked behind the glass doors in the butler's pantry. I can see my favorite pattern with the birds and flowers. "Singapore Bird," Grandma told me. The top of the silver sink sparkles. It's where the china is rinsed after the plates are cleared.

Grandma pushes the swinging door to the dining room. It has a little window made of yellow-and-green glass.

Philippe follows close behind and sneezes.

The long white curtains in the dining room are like giant sails as the breeze from Lake Superior blows through the open windows. The room smells like freshly mowed grass and the flowers in the formal garden.

Grandma kneels on the fancy rug; it covers the whole floor. The giant dinner table is made from a tree. "Mahogany," Grandma has told me.

"Look here," she says.

I'm barely as tall as the table but I'm taller than Philippe. I look closely. There's another doorbell under the edge of the table!

Philippe sits by the marble fireplace. He watches Grandma as she stands and straightens her dress. Then she walks to the other end of the table and she points again.

I run to look. It's another one! The doorbells are everywhere.

"What does it do?" I ask.

Grandma rubs her finger across the shiny white button. "It lets the maids know that we're ready for the next course," she says. "Sometimes it's to let them know that we need something."

"I can't hear it," I say.

"That's because it rings in the kitchen."

Grandma presses the pearly white button. It sounds like a baby bumblebee.

Caroline magically appears from behind the swinging door. She has a light gray uniform with a white lace collar and cuffs. White apron strings are tied in a perfect bow. She smiles and walks through the dining room without saying a word.

"Grandma, do people come when you press the doorbell?"

"Only if we're at dinner."

"Are there doorbells in the breakfast room?"

Grandma stands and runs her hand down the front of her dress like she's ironing.

"Let's go look," she says.

The breakfast table is made of carved black wood. Grandma calls it sugi, a cedar tree from Japan. I peek under the edges of the table. No doorbells.

Grandma pulls out the big black chair at the head of the table and she sits down. All of a sudden there's a sound, very soft, like a buzzer. It's coming from the butler's pantry. Grandma moves her foot up and down like she's keeping time to music. I see a little bump underneath the dark brown rug with pink flowers. Grandma's foot is heavy but I use both hands to move it to the side and then I peek under the corner of the rug. A piece of shiny metal with a button in the middle is right on top of the green tiles on the floor.

"A magic button!" I say, as I crawl out from under the table. I stand and smooth the front of my dress with my hand, just like Grandma.

The sun shines through the acorn and oak leaf design in the glass windows. "The little acorn works very hard," Grandma says. "It must have patience in order to find its strength and power to grow into a tall oak tree."

A small brass cup hangs on a hook near the faucet in the wall. A green metal turtle covers the opening where the water goes down the drain.

Grandma smiles as she gives the big ferns a drink.

I lean over the edge of the big clay pot and watch as the water disappears into the black dirt.

"Come with me, please," Grandma says.

Philíppe and I follow through the formal dining room. I stop and wrap myself in the soft folds of the purple velvet drapes with the gold thread, pretending it's a princess robe.

Philíppe sniffs my black leather shoes.

"Where's Suzanne?" Grandma says. She likes to play the game.

I giggle and twirl my way out.

Holding the princess robe by the hem, I wrap it around my shoulders and walk forward, pretending it's a long train.

Caroline is down the hall twirling a feather duster over the gold frame of a painting just in case there are spider webs or dust. She glides across the fancy carpets like a ballerina with a fairy wand.

Philíppe runs down the hallway to meet her.

I finger the charms on Grandma's bracelet as she leads the way to Great-grandfather's study where he signed important papers and smoked cigars. The little room is right across from the library with all the books and paintings and the big windows where we watch the ships on Lake Superior.

Just inside the study, Grandma points to the middle of the wall right next to the brick fireplace. It's another white button!

"If my father needed anything," Grandma says. "He would ring the staff."

"Did they come?" I ask.

"They were always ready," Grandma says.

It's afternoon at Grandma's summer house in Wisconsin. I know it's called Swiftwater Farm because of the rapids of the Brule River that flow along the banks of the wooded property. The name is printed in blue on the white stationery in the antique desk in the living room. The name is sewn in red and blue on the towels that hang in the bathrooms.

Grandma and I stand in the doorway of her bedroom. It's on the second floor, next to the small bathroom with the slanted ceiling. The bedroom windows have white curtains and cream shades with tiny rings to pull them down. Outside the windows, the flower boxes are filled with red geraniums. A light green double bed is next to the painted white wall.

"I like my bed facing the woods," Grandma says. She peeks through the tiny window. "The twinkling stars smile at me and I can hear the sound of the rapids." She stops and listens for a minute. I hear the water rushing over the rocks, too.

A dark green wooden dresser is next to the wall. The light blue table has a small lamp and a pretty white shade. Sometimes Grandma falls asleep with the light on when she reads. The door to the tiny closet is open. Tan and yellow cotton dresses hang like curtains but I can still see the brown-and-white leather shoes on the wood floor.

"Sensible shoes," Grandma says. "Very comfortable."

My red canvas PF Flyers have red rubber that goes over the toes. A bright green rubber patch over the heel has the initials PF in white. I'm sure it means that I can run Pretty Fast. "Grandma, my shoes are magic," I say. "They bring me to you."

"I'm so glad," she says.

"Do you always wear a dress?" I ask. I have never seen her wear pants, ever.

"Yes, except for times as a girl and young woman when I wore wide-legged pants that looked like a skirt."

"Like culottes?"

"Just like that," Grandma says. "And my swimming costume had blousy pants."

"What color?"

"Navy blue with a striped collar," she says. "It had short sleeves with white liners and round blue-and-white buttons up the front." Grandma touches her belly button and her heart to show me. "Sometimes, I wore leggings under a skirt. Do you remember the picture of my brother Robert and me, hiking on the glacier in Canada?"

"You had a long stick in the snow," I say.

"The walking stick," Grandma says.

"So you didn't fall."

Grandma nods. Then she looks at the ceiling like she's checking for cracks. She thinks for a minute. "I used to ski jump at the Chester Ski Slide and I wore wide black pants." She bends her knees and brings her arms way back like she's going to jump. Her cheeks are puffed out like a snowman and she makes a sound like the wind.

I crouch down, too. My arms are stretched behind me like bird wings. I can almost feel the breeze.

"Sometimes we would even toboggan down the slide," Grandma says.

"Was it fun?"

"Lots of fun," Grandma says. She rolls her lips like she just put on lipstick even though she hasn't. "Now I always wear a dress. Even when I canoe and when I bait a hook at Angleton's pond."

"Does your dress ever fly up?"

"No, it hasn't happened. I'm very careful."

"You are a lady, Grandma."

"Why, thank you," Grandma says.

We make our way down the short hallway, hand in hand. Past the linen closet where the beach towels decorated with starfish are kept, along with the folded sheets and pillowcases and rows of bath towels.

The wood floors of the old farmhouse creak.

The bedroom next to Grandma's room is pink, as pink as the bedroom at Glensheen. This bedroom is smaller. Curtains with tiny pink flowers cover the windows that open from the middle, like butterfly wings. They stay open with a thin metal stick connected to the windowsill. The bright blue sky and puffy white clouds are right outside the windows. I can hear the wind whistle and I smell the fir trees. It's so peaceful and quiet. I think God lives here.

The little bed has carved flower petals on the pink headboard and pink-and-blue flowers near the curved top, just like the wildflowers I see in the woods: bluebells, pink fireweed, and pink lady's slipper. A dark pink dresser barely fits in the corner beneath the tin mirror from Mexico. A thin strip of pink wood follows the bottom of the wall. A small rug, light pink and bright blue, covers the floor.

"I know something we can do," Grandma says. "So you always know I am here."

"A game?" I ask.

"Like a message," Grandma says. "So you will feel safe."

"How do you do it?"

Grandma sits on the little bed and the mattress springs squeak. She touches the white plaster wall with her fingertips. "I will knock on my side of the wall three times like this." Grandma knocks once...a second time...and then a third time. "It means, 'I love you.' The walls are very thin so you will be able to hear me."

"Okay," I say.

"Then you knock once...and then a second time, which means, 'How...much?'"

"I can do it!" I knock twice on the wall to show her.

"Exactly right," Grandma says.

"Then what?" I ask.

"I knock once, long and strong, which means, 'Lots.' Do you want to try it?"

"Okay!" I say.

I watch as Grandma leaves the room. I know that I am safe if she is near. I think about telling her about Mom's pink Studebaker station wagon catching fire when we were here earlier this summer. My little brother Andy and I were in the back seat ready to go into town. Mom got in the car and slammed the door. The white collar of her dress had little points on each end. She started the engine.

I smelled something burning like a forest fire. Dark black smoke curled into the air.

"There's smoke and flames!" Dad yelled as he came running from the house.

"Now what?" Mom yelled back. "Get the hose!"

Andy started to cry.

I grabbed the silver handle on the door and pushed down hard. The door opened and Andy and I scrambled out.

But Mom yelled, "Get back in the car!"

Dad and Mom kept yelling at each other. I couldn't hear the words anymore because I was so scared. Dad's face was red. He opened the hood of the car and grabbed the bright green hose that looked like a snake. He sprayed the engine with water. The engine sizzled. The black smoke made me think of *Puff, the Magic Dragon*. He lives by the sea. There is no sea at Brule. There is a river.

Elna, the cook, ran out the screened door of the kitchen. Her light brown hair was flying in the wind. Her short legs moved fast so she could get to Andy and me. She grabbed us before we got back in the car.

Mom and Dad didn't look as Elna hurried us into the house. They were still fighting.

Andy sat down on the living room floor to play Lincoln Logs with Steve and Pete.

Elna held my hand as she led me to the porch off the kitchen. She sat in the big blue chair that has cracks in the paint and she pulled up a little stool so I could sit beside her.

My hands were trembling as I watched her shuck the shiny green peas into a light blue bowl. I picked up a small green pea pod and looked closely at the seam. Elna placed her fingers over mine and together we made the seam snap. I wanted to ask her to be my mother but I was too shy.

Grandma is here now. I don't want to tell her the story. I might get in trouble with Mom and Dad and they might not bring me to visit. I want Grandma to be happy when we're together. It's our special time.

My ear is next to the cool white wall. I wait and listen.

Three knocks come through, loud and clear.

I hold my breath and make two firm knocks.

Grandma's final knock flies back.

The blue-and-yellow flowered dress has sewing at the top. Mom says it's smocking. She calls the dress a name, Florence Eiseman, and she tells people that it's from Dayton's department store. Dad says it's too expensive. My little sisters, Becky and Heather, and I have matching outfits.

Mom looks straight ahead as she drives me to Breck School. We have a new car, a white station wagon with red seats and dark brown wood on the sides, because the pink station wagon caught on fire. I remember the smoke.

"Are we there yet?" I ask. It's my first day of kindergarten.

"We'll be there when we get there!" Mom snaps. A minute later she stops the car and says, "Open the door."

I look for a school but all I see are tall trees and a wide black road. I don't know what to do.

"Open the door!" Mom screams. "You'll be late."

I struggle with the door handle but it finally opens and I stumble out.

Mom pulls the door closed from the inside and then she drives away.

My chin trembles but I don't cry.

The cars on the road go fast.

I turn around and all I can see is water far below and a dusty riverbank on the other side. No boats.

A yellow brick building is on the other side of the road. I think maybe the building is the school. The boys are wearing gray pants with blue stripes down the sides. I wonder why they are all dressed alike. Maybe they are brothers.

I look at the road again. No cars.

I run as fast as I can to reach the other side. My heart is pounding.

The boys are going into the building. I try to catch up, but I can't see them anymore.

A tall man comes running toward me. He has straight black hair and glasses. I wonder if his neck hurts because of his tight white collar.

"My name is Canon Henderson," he says as he gasps for air. He looks like a giant but he bends down so I can see his face. "What's your name?" he asks.

"Suzanne LeRoy," I say. I'm not supposed to talk to strangers but I tell.

"You must be in kindergarten," he says. His big hand feels like my brother's catcher's mitt. We walk inside the school together, past the tall gray lockers that look like soldiers.

The kindergarten classroom has big windows. I can see the playground outside. Dark green swing sets, jungle gyms, and a sand box. Inside, the boys and girls are coloring at a long table on the other side of the sunny room. Crayon drawings of birds are taped to the walls. A black bird has red and yellow on its wings. It looks like a little cape. I wonder if the bird is cold.

"Red-winged blackbird," the teacher says. The lady has black curly hair and a brown skirt with a stiff petticoat like a square dance dress.

I wonder if it twirls.

The kids run to the middle of the room and they sit in a circle on the floor. A little girl has long brown hair tied in a bow. It looks like sunshine and matches her dress. She smiles and pats the floor where she wants me to be.

I sit next to the nice little girl.

I wonder if she had to run across the road.

Grandma has a little house in Tucson, Arizona. It doesn't have a name. She goes there to see the cactus and the desert and the sunshine. There are no lakes or rivers but there's a patio made of pretty rocks and stones, a white wall, a little black gate with a curly top, and lots of plants in clay pots.

"Saguaro, very prickly. Mustn't touch," Grandma says as we walk past the tall green cactus. It's just outside her house with the shutters on the windows and clay tiles on the roof.

Grandma winks at me as we make our way down the hallway.

I hold a finger over one eye and I blink with the other, so I can wink back.

In the small bedroom with the white walls, there's a beautiful dress spread out on the bed.

"It's a special dress called a dirndl," Grandma says. "It means young girl."

"Like Heidi's dress!" I say. I remember the story of the little girl who lives in the mountains.

The black skirt is soft, just like the velvet drapes at Glensheen. "Pretty flowers," I say. The tiny threads are the color of buttercups, blue-bells, green grass, roses, and the whitest snow. I can almost feel the tiny flowers in my hand.

I lean over and sniff like I do in the garden or the woods. But there's no smell.

"There's a lady coming to paint your picture," Grandma says. She helps me button the white blouse with the short puffed sleeves.

I raise my hands as she holds the pretty dress over my head and then she carefully pulls it down. A ribbon, as red as a cardinal, is laced within the dress and tied in a small bow at my waist. I twirl the end around my finger.

I unbuckle the straps of my black leather shoes and place them beneath my white socks, but inside the shoes. Grandma watches, not saying a word.

"Slip-ons," I say. "Like big girls."

"What a good idea," Grandma says. She looks at my light brown bangs. The double cowlicks always bounce up when I try to comb my hair. "You look beautiful," she says.

The living room has white walls with framed pictures and dark red tiles on the floor. A lady is setting up a stand with a big board. Grandma calls it an easel.

"Mrs. Loney," Grandma says. The lady bends down and smiles. She has brown hair, tan pants, and brown shoes. Her big straw hat hangs on the side of the sofa.

"Hello, Suzanne," she says.

"Hi," I whisper.

I climb onto the seat of the tall chair and turn around. It's scratchy against the back of my legs so I sit cross-legged and straighten the front of my dress.

"My father gave this to me when I was little," Grandma says. "It's an art book for children."

A dried leaf is hiding between the pages.

"Gingko," Grandma says. She picks the leaf up by the little stem. "Look at the tiny gold pleats." Sunlight shines through the little fan. Grandma places it between the pages again to keep it safe.

"Pencil writing, Grandma," I say as I turn to the first page of the book.

"To Elisabeth, Love Papa," she says as she traces each word with her fingertip.

The lady behind the big board is busy painting.

After a while Grandma picks up her camera. "To help the artist remember what you look like."

I look straight into the camera and smile.

"Good job," Grandma says.

I turn and kneel on the seat of the chair. Then I reach one foot down until I feel the floor, and then the other.

"Would you like to see?" the artist says as she leans to the side.

I nod and come closer. I see pencil lines and paint, a little girl's face.

"I have something to show you," Grandma says when our family visits her at Glensheen. She takes my hand and we walk across the hall to Great-grandfather Chester's study, where she reads her mail and writes letters. Sometimes she likes to look at the tall green trees in front of the house.

The ceiling of the room has wood beams made from trees called chestnut and cypress. The big copper light looks like lilies. Grandma told me about Great-grandfather and the iron ore and copper mining. His favorite flower was the water lily. I see it in the pool of the marble dolphin fountain where the goldfish swim. Grandma says there's another kind of lily near the copper mines in Arizona. It's a garlic lily.

A small brick fireplace has a copper bucket filled with little pieces of wood. The maids use the broom to sweep the ashes into the metal dustpan.

Grandma points to the wall covered with grasscloth. I touched it once and it felt like straw. A painting in the middle of the wall has a gold frame. Long wires from the ceiling hold it up so it doesn't fall and crash. A little light above the top of the frame shines on the painting.

I look up and tilt my head, studying the little girl in the black velvet dress with tiny flowers.

"Grandma," I say. "That's me!"

"It's very special to me and so are you," she says. "You are my first granddaughter."

CHAPTER II

HOPE

Hope is faith holding out its hand in the dark.
—George Isles

It's dark outside. The white linoleum of the kitchen floor feels cold against my bare feet. The only light turned on is over the pink sink at our home in Minneapolis.

"Sign the check!" Dad screams. A long piece of yellow paper waves like a flag in his hand.

"I'm not signing it!" Mom yells back.

Mom and Dad don't see me. I think I can sneak away, but it's too late.

Dad's large arm and hand fly through the air. I hear a sound like a tree branch breaking in two.

Mom's cheek is the color of a dark red apple, much darker than the light pink sink.

I grab the sides of my Lanz nightgown with the tiny flowers and lace trim and I run as fast as I can. Up the stairs, across the short landing, then four more steps, stubbing my toe on the last one.

Hopping on one foot I reach the doorway of my bedroom, first door on the left. I run across the oriental rug and I jump into my bed and grab Raggedy Ann. Then I jump out the other side. I leave the closet door open just a crack so I can see the light from downstairs. My hands tremble as I hold Raggedy Ann close to my chest.

"Don't be afraid," I whisper. I touch her dress where the little heart on her cloth body says I LOVE YOU. I can't see it in the dark but I know it's there. "I'll protect you," I say. "No one will ever hurt you."

Bob, the head gardener at Glensheen, is as tall as the Jolly Green Giant. He smells like sunshine and he gives Grandma beautiful purple-and-yellow pansies that float in the finger bowls we use at dinner. His large hands put tiny green sprouts in the warm dirt so they can grow. He does not hit.

James, the chauffeur, holds out his hand so Grandma doesn't fall. The maids use their hands to clean the house so Grandma sees beautiful things. Caroline and Frieda hold the shiny silver trays of food as they serve from the left and clear from the right.

Anna, the cook, makes pies and cakes on the marble pastry board.

Ole holds the black shovel as he scoops coal into the furnace so the house stays warm for Grandma. Pete and I watch Ole make repairs at the carpenter's bench across from the furnace room.

My older brothers, Steve and Pete, wrestle but they never hit. They pull out Grandma's chair at dinner. They are polite. They have manners.

Grandma's hands are pink and soft and they hold my hands so I feel safe and loved.

Carl, the caretaker at Brule, cleans fish with his hands. He fixes the benches and he mows the bright green grass. He paints the farmhouse and makes it beautiful for Grandma.

Elna makes Indian pudding and cakes with white frosting topped with marshmallow flowers and real pansies for decoration.

I go to first grade and I worry about the yelling and hitting at home. My teacher, Mrs. Ramsey, has brown hair and glasses. She smells like cotton candy. We read about Dick and Jane. They have a cat named Puff and a dog, named Spot. I like to read about the happy children.

I watch Dad's hands. He never hits me. I try to be brave but I'm too afraid to tell anyone what happens in our house.

My head pounds and it aches. The school nurse calls Mom but she doesn't come for a long time. I rest on the little white bed with the mattress as soft as a cloud. The nurse's office is safe and quiet.

Dr. Sterrie says he can't find anything wrong. He asks if anything is bothering me. I shake my head, no.

I think about running away but Grandma's house is too far.

I tie the laces of my PF Flyers and sit cross-legged on the oriental rug in my bedroom.

"Fly me away," I whisper. It never does. I ask the rug to try a little harder.

Carl Pearson used to have twelve cows in Maple, Wisconsin. Then he worked the ore docks in Duluth, right by the big loaders and ships. Now he takes care of Swiftwater Farm for Grandma. Carl smells like the burnt marshmallows we made over the campfire. He carries a pack of Camel cigarettes in the pocket of his plaid shirt but I never see him smoke.

"Can we go to the dump?" Pete asks.

"Yup," Carl says with a twinkle in his eye. "Just gettin' ready to go to town."

Grandma knows we go to the dump with Carl and she doesn't mind. He has strict rules for safety.

"Okay, rules at the dump," Carl tells us each time before we leave. "Always keep the doors locked. Always keep the windows up. No talking unless it's a whisper. We do not unload garbage unless the bears are gone. If we see bears and they get upset we need to skedaddle. Any questions?"

"Nope," Pete and I say.

Carl drives the red Ford truck down the long driveway. A cloud of dust flies through the air as the big tires go fast on the dirt road.

Woolly, the Lassie dog, runs after us halfway. Then he stops and trots back to Carl's log cabin just like he always does when he can't keep up with the truck. Pete and I turn around and check to make sure that Woolly gets home.

"Congdon Road," Carl says. He points to the small green sign.

My PF Flyers are wet from the morning dew. Light blue pedal pushers go just below my knees. Tiny goose bumps cover my legs.

"Fire risk is low," Pete says as he reads the sign up ahead. He blows into his hands to keep them warm.

Carl follows the twisty dirt road in the forest. He holds the big black steering wheel with one hand. It's strong enough to keep the truck going straight on the road. His other hand covers the round black knob of the long stick that looks like a tree growing out of the floor.

"Does Grandma ever drive the truck?" I ask.

"Not that I know of," Carl says.

"Grandma could do it," I say. "She had a race car!"

"She did?" Carl says.

"A Bearcat," I say. "Grandma showed me a picture. There was a little round windshield and a tire on the back. And a silver stick shift and a crank to start it!"

"A Stutz Bearcat?" Carl asks.

"Yeah!" I say. "Grandma said she wore a long coat to keep her dress clean. And she had a hat and a scarf. And you know what else?"

"What else?" Carl says.

"There was an electric car. Aunt Marjorie drove it. Grandma, too."

"Yup, I heard about that one," Carl says.

"It had a tiller," I say. "A big stick for steering."

"Did not," Pete says.

"Did so," I say. "Go ask Grandma."

I feel secretly proud. Grandma told me about the cars when she drove her maroon station wagon to the fish hatchery in Brule and the cheese factory in Iron River.

Pete looks out the window, as Carl turns onto Highway 2. We pass Denny's tiny grocery store. My mouth waters as I think of the penny candy: Pixy Stix, strawberry licorice wheels, rock candy, and jawbreakers.

Carl slows down and points to the small green street sign. "Dump Road," he says. The metal gate to the dump is wide open. Carl drives in and pulls to the side of the road.

A big dug-out hole is as big as Grandma's summer house. Boxes, an old tricycle, and paper bags are tumbled off to the side. Flies buzz around the garbage.

Pete and I squirm in our seats.

"Okay, quiet please," Carl whispers. We wait for a few seconds. Carl points.

Two black bears are ripping open cardboard boxes like it's Christmas. Suddenly, a third bear shows up. He sniffs at an old tire, pushes it over with his nose, and paws the ground and snorts.

We all press close against the windows.

Two of the bears walk on all fours toward the truck.

Carl shifts into reverse.

The bears stop and watch us. Then one bear sits down. The other bear scratches his side and sniffs the air.

"Smokey the Bear might be here," Carl whispers.

I look at the third bear but I don't see the special hat that Smokey wears. Maybe the forest ranger knows where he lives.

A fawn runs by and stops, trembling in the cool morning air. The bears don't notice. I look for Bambi's friends, Thumper the Rabbit and Flower the Skunk. But they're not here.

"Run Bambi, run!" I whisper. The deer jumps into the forest as if she heard me.

"Close call," Carl says. But I know Bambi is safe.

Grandma's small navy blue hat matches her dress. A blue leather purse, with a little brass snap, matches her shoes. A ring with blue stones matches her outfit. She carries a pair of short white gloves in her hand. "You can tell the time of day by the length of a lady's gloves," she says.

"You're pretty, Grandma," I say.

"Why, thank you," she says. "So are you." My white dress has blue smocking at the top. The tip of my finger fits in one of the puckers.

Grandma picks up her gloves. "Ready to go?" she asks.

I nod.

James opens the big front door at Glensheen. The green Cadillac is right outside. It sparkles in the sun.

"Lonsdale Building," Grandma says.

James drives past the black metal gates that look like rows of spears. He stops and looks both ways. London Road is a busy street.

It's a quick trip. James stops the car close to the curb and he holds the door open as we step out.

Grandma and I walk through the front lobby. The floors are shiny like glass. We step into the metal elevator and the door closes. I push the button with the little arrow. The elevator goes up, no bumps. The door opens. A big door is right across the hallway.

"Congdon Office Corporation," Grandma says as she points to the black letters on the glass. Then she turns the brass doorknob and opens the door.

A glass jar on the desk is filled with candy. "You may have one piece," Grandma says.

The lady behind the desk has bright pink lipstick and curly brown hair. She pulls up a chair right beside her desk and pats the seat.

I roll my lips pretending that I have pink lipstick too, but I hold Grandma's hand and wait.

"Hello," Grandma says to Mr. Van Evera and Mr. Adams. The men have gray suits and shiny black shoes. They smile at me and shake Grandma's hand. They call her Elisabeth. She calls them Bill and Sals. They are friends.

"Hello, Suzanne," Mr. Van Evera says. "How are you?"

"Good," I whisper.

"I won't be long," Grandma says.

I watch as she goes into another room with the men. The door closes behind them.

The lady behind the desk holds the glass candy jar down low so I can see. I pick one Hershey's Kiss. The thin white paper with blue writing looks like smoke coming from the top of the tin foil. I carefully unwrap the candy and press the wrapper into a tiny ball. The sweet chocolate melts in my mouth.

I can smell the lady's flowery perfume as I climb onto the chair, one knee at a time.

"Who are you?" I ask.

"Dorothy," she says.

"That's the girl in the *Wizard of Oz*," I say. "Her dog is Toto."

"Yes, that's right."

"Did Great-grandfather Chester come here?"

"I think he came in to see if everyone else was working. He was very busy traveling around the country doing business."

"Mining?" I ask.

"Yes. Many other things, too."

"Was he the boss?"

"Yes, and he met with other businessmen. There were many meetings."

I point to the door where Grandma went with the men in gray suits. "What do they do in there?" I ask.

"They talk business."

"Iron ore?"

"Sometimes," Dorothy says.

"Is the iron ore in there?"

"No, that stays outside or in the ships."

"I see ships when we come to visit Grandma," I say.

"That's right. The loaders put the iron ore in the hull," Dorothy says. "That's the bottom of the boat. The iron ore stays there while the ship sails."

"Grandma says iron make steel."

"Yes, it does."

I look at Dorothy's tiny brown belt. It holds up her skirt. "What do you do?" I ask.

"I help the trustees."

"What do they do?"

"They take care of accounts and property around the country, like Glensheen where you visit your grandmother. They're in touch with all the Congdon family."

"I'm a Congdon," I say. "Grandma, too."

"That's right," Dorothy says.

The door creaks.

Grandma walks out with the men in gray suits. They're smiling.

"Grandma, what's in there?" I whisper, as I point to the door.

"Let's go see," she says as she takes my hand. We walk through the doorway and I peek inside the room. A large wooden desk is the color of honey. Grandma points to the small flowers carved on each side.

The tips of my fingers fit inside the petals.

"Your great-grandfather's desk," she says.

The yellow sofa in the library is soft as a marshmallow. Grandma's arm is wrapped around my shoulders like a warm cape.

"You were born in Duluth," she says. "Just over four years ago at St. Luke's Hospital."

"In the night?" I ask.

"Around nine o'clock in the morning," Grandma says. "On a cold day." She rubs her arms like she is shivering.

"Were there snowflakes?"

"I think there were a few."

Grandma bends her elbows and holds her hands out wide. "You were about this big. Eight pounds."

"Did I cry?"

"Yes, a little bit."

"Did you adopt me?" I ask. I know that Grandma adopted Mom and Aunt Jennifer when they were babies because she told me.

"No, because you have a mother and a father and a home where you live."

"You're my Grandma," I say. I lean my head against her chest and she holds me close.

"Two weeks after you were born you were baptized right around the corner in the living room." I turn to look but I just see the hallway.

"Did you hold me?" I ask.

"Yes, I did," Grandma says.

"Just you and me?"

"No, your mother and father, your older brothers Stephen and Peter, and my sister Marjorie and her husband."

"That's the cross lady."

"Who?" Grandma says.

"Aunt Marjorie."

"No, no, she's not cross," Grandma says. "She's actually very funny. Do you remember how we ate pizza at her house, right down the road?"

"Oh, yeah! In the summer, we sat on the fancy rug," I say. "I didn't spill. Steve and Pete ate pizza too."

"That's right."

"Was your other sister there?"

"When was that?" Grandma says.

"When I was baptized."

"No, Helen wasn't there."

"She's Annie Oakley."

"Annie Oakley?"

"In the pictures, Grandma. She shoots guns and rides horses. She rode Dexter. You, too."

"Yes, that's right," Grandma says.

"Did I wear a pretty dress?" I ask.

"Yes, your baptismal dress was white with dainty white lace. A long dress past your feet."

"Kinda like a formal?"

"Well, a very pretty dress for a formal occasion."

"Now you, Grandma," I say.

"I was born at home on a Sunday, late at night on April 22, 1894," she says. "The white house we have driven by with James."

"With the round part sticking up?"

"Yes, the turret," Grandma says. "I was baptized at home but I was two years old."

"Were you in a long dress?"

"A little longer than yours. It was a cream color with a lace collar and a pretty pin."

"Grandma, where were you?" I ask. "When you held me."

"I stood right in front of the marble fireplace."

I can see the black lines in the stone as we make our way down the hallway.

Grandma stops and points to a design on one of the chandeliers in the living room. "Scallop shell," she says.

It looks like a little mermaid bed.

"The shells have a special meaning. Birth and baptism, and a guardian angel called Raphael."

"That's a good story," I say. Grandma gently squeezes my hand.

Tonight there is a dinner party at our house in Minneapolis. The people who help are dressed in black. They fill shiny platters with food and set them on the table, which seems as long as a football field. Tall white candles have flames like stars.

"Put on your new pajamas and go to bed," Mom says to my brothers and sisters and me. We scurry up the stairs, each one trying to be first.

Soon there are people laughing and talking downstairs. There's a clinking of glasses and the sound of forks and knives against the china plates.

I know they'll be coming soon. It's happened before. Mom and Dad bring strangers upstairs and they stare at my brothers and sisters and me.

I can hear the heavy feet on the stairway. Laughing. Loud voices.

The light switch is flipped on.

I face the window, pretending I am asleep in my canopy bed.

The strangers talk loudly.

"Oh, this house is beautiful!"

"How do you keep everything so neat with all these children?"

"Are these antiques?"

"Over one hundred fifty years old," Mom says.

I know that we are very poor because we have such old furniture. The only things in this room that are really mine are the baby teeth that I save in the pewter inkwell with the dark red feather. No one ever looks in there.

The room is dark again. I roll over.

Mom and dad take the strangers down the hall.

I hope my little sisters are asleep.

Pete and Andy run across the cobblestones at the edge of Lake Superior. They stumble over the rocks of every size, shape, and color as they race to Tischer Creek.

I skip alongside Grandma. Her tan-and-white shoes match her dress with the little brown leather belt. "Driftwood," she says. The gray wood is scattered among the rocks beneath our feet.

Grandma bends down and picks up one special rock.

"Can you see the lines?" she asks. "Like rings inside a tree. Lake Superior agate, very special."

Pete comes running. He leans over so he can see the rock in the palm of her hand.

"Quartz," Grandma says. "The red, orange, and yellow colors are from iron." She hands the agate to Pete.

"Thanks, Grandma!" he says. "I'm gonna save it." He reaches far down in his pocket, takes his hand out minus the stone, and pats his pocket for good measure. A gray gull hovers above his head. The air smells like fish. Pete picks up another stone and hurls it across the glistening water. Three skips.

Grandma and I search for the perfect smooth flat stone. Grandma finds one and hands it to me. The edges are warm from the sun.

"Pancake," I say.

Grandma places her right hand over mine and then she gently reaches back. Her strong arm and hand flick forward. The stone flies through the air and skips four times through the sparkly blue water. As light as a fairy not wanting to get her toes wet.

CHAPTER III

FAMILY TRUST

Life is not meant to be easy, my child;
but take courage—it can be delightful.
— George Bernard Shaw

Every year long yellow pieces of paper come in the mail at Christmas time. I know they're presents for my brothers and sisters and me. The scalloped edge is a cartoon ocean wave. The words "Congdon Office Corporation" are printed in the upper left corner. My name, Suzanne LeRoy, is typed on the front.

"Sign the check," Dad says.

I lean against the big oak desk in the den and turn the paper over, looking for the special line where I sign my name. I blow on the ink so it won't smear just like Grandma does when she writes letters.

Mom grabs the check from my hand. "It goes to me!" she screams.

"It's mine!" Dad yells.

The rumpled paper is a present for me but Mom and Dad are fighting over it like they always do. I wonder where the check goes. The same thing happens when a check comes on my birthday.

"Go to your room!" Mom yells.

I bolt and race up the stairs as fast as I can.

"My mother sends the checks! It's my money," Mom screams at Dad.

I catch my breath as I rummage through the bottom drawer of my dresser. The toe of one of my white ankle socks has the coins from my allowance. Nickels, dimes, quarters, and pennies fall on the floor. I count each one. My savings are all there, $1.23. I know that it needs to stay hidden.

I write a thank-you note to Grandma in my best handwriting. I want to tell her that I don't know what happens to the checks but I don't want to get in trouble with Mom and Dad. I think about writing a letter to Mr. Van Evera or Mr. Maine at the Congdon Office. They would know where the money goes. But I don't because Mom and Dad fight all the time and it's always about money.

Grandma told me how hard Great-grandfather Chester worked when he was growing up. He had a job in a lumberyard and a grocery store because his father died when Great-grandfather was fifteen. He was the oldest and he took care of his mother, a little brother, and a little sister. Two other brothers and a sister died one year before from scarlet fever.

"My father went to school and he studied hard," Grandma said. "He saved his money so he could pass it on to others in the family."

"Like a present?" I asked.

"Just like that," she said.

Bills are piled high on the dining room table at home. I know that we are poor but I don't know how to make it better.

"I need a note for school because I was sick yesterday," I say.

Dad pushes away the lined piece of notebook paper. Instead, he tears off the top of a Rice Krispies cereal box and writes the note on the gray side of the box top. He laughs as he hands me the scruffy cardboard.

"I have paper," I say. "Please write it on the paper."

"No, take this!" Dad yells.

It isn't funny. My cheeks are on fire. I've seen Dad write cereal box top notes for my brothers. I don't ever want to be sick again. Being poor is something I already know. Now I think I understand it even more. We need to save the paper.

"Hurry up and get in the car," Dad says.

The soft black top of the green Triumph sports car is down and Dad makes the little car go fast. I can barely hold on to the edges of the slippery brown seat. My hair is blown by the wind again and again.

"Mississippi River," Dad says as he points to the left. His tie flies in the wind.

Suddenly the car swerves like an S, and I slide into the door.

Dad looks at me and he laughs.

"I don't like that!" I say. "Don't do it."

"Oh, stop it!" Dad says. He pretends to drive over the cliff, again and again. He laughs each time I grab the seat to hold on.

The wind is so cold there are goose bumps on my legs. Dad keeps playing the game. I don't say anything. I know he won't stop if I do.

Dexter's white name plate with the black letters still hangs above his stall even though he's been gone a long time. I practice saying the names of the horses that used to live here: "Dynamo, Sangamo, Dick, and Harry," as I run my fingers over the lacquered blanket rails in the stable at Glensheen.

Footsteps echo throughout the carriage house.

"They were quarter horses," James says. "And Morgan horses."

I turn around and smile. "They pulled the carriages and sleighs," I say.

James nods. "Sometimes they pulled ice from the lake."

James used to be a footman, then a butler. Now he's Grandma's chauffeur. He drives the emerald Cadillac and calls it "Congdon green." The Pierce-Arrow, Stutz Bearcat, and electric car with the charging station are gone.

"Grandma said she tied Dexter to a toboggan," I say. "He ran off."

James looks at me and chuckles.

The smooth leather bridles and blinkers have Great-grandfather's sparkling silver initials, CAC, for Chester Adgate Congdon. The saddles, harnesses, carriage whips, and fly nets are neatly arranged in the tack room. The air smells like the saddle soap that James uses to keep the leather shiny and clean.

"Good morning, Miss Elisabeth," James says.

Grandma always lets the staff know where she is. She must have called on the intercom in the house. James and Bob, the head gardener, are the only ones who call Grandma, "Miss Elisabeth." They've known her a long time. The rest of the staff call her, "Miss Congdon."

"Good morning, James," Grandma says. "Lovely day."

I run to meet her as she walks past the red-and-white gasoline pump with the long black hose. It's just outside the carriage house door.

"Hi, Grandma," I say.

"Would you like to see the carriages?" she asks.

I nod.

Grandma takes my hand as we walk through the wood-and-glass sliding doors with the diamond shaped design. We climb the stairs surrounded by white tile walls as we make our way to the second floor.

The big black wheel of the hand-operated elevator for the carriages and sleighs is high above us. There's a smell of old leather.

James follows to protect us in case we trip or fall. He always wears a matching hat and jacket.

Grandma walks past the old carriages and sleighs, admiring each one as she says the name. "Two-passenger Brewster Victoria. Studebaker Utility Wagon." She stops for a few seconds to look at the Russian sleigh. Then she comes to a big black carriage with four wheels and open sides. "Two-passenger Phaeton," she says. Her pale pink nail polish sparkles in the sunlight as she slides her fingertips along the edge of the black fabric seat.

"May I, Miss Elisabeth?" James asks.

Grandma places her hand in his and she steps into the carriage. She motions for me to follow.

"Suzanne," James says. He holds out his large hand.

I place my hand in his and I step into the beautiful black carriage. I imagine the horses with shiny coats and polished leather harnesses. I can almost see the gray swirls of horse breath.

"Did you feel like a princess in the olden days?" I ask.

"Oh, yes," Grandma says.

I pretend I am a princess, too.

Dad and my brothers stand in their dark suits as Grandma walks into the library at Glensheen. Her dark green dress has long sleeves, and there's a pin that looks like a gold basket filled with flowers made of pretty stones. Mom is wearing a green linen dress. My sisters and I have matching light blue dresses with red and yellow tulips and bright green stems. Formal dress for dinner is Grandma's only request.

The portraits of Great-grandfather Chester and Great-grandmother Clara make it seem as if they are dressed for dinner, too. Great-grandfather's three-piece suit is black and his white shirt has a tall, stiff collar and a dark tie. His gray hair and thick gray moustache are neatly trimmed. He's holding a pair of wire-rimmed glasses.

"The red carnation in his lapel represents the fresh flower that he gave my mother every day," Grandma says. "It came from our own greenhouse."

Great-grandmother's gray hair is loosely pulled off her face. There's a hint of pink in her cheeks. Her black dress has long sleeves and she's wearing a matching choker. Her gold wedding band sparkles.

"Did Great-grandfather Chester think she was pretty?" I ask.

"Oh, yes," Grandma says. "She caught his eye during algebra class when they were in college."

Caroline silently appears. She stands beside the pocket doors made of two types of wood. Mahogany on one side matches the library, and oak on the other side matches the hallway. "Miss Congdon, dinner is served," she says.

Fancy rugs cover the floor, just like the magic carpets from the place called Persia. I pretend the hallway is a beautiful forest of white oak and the glow from the Quezal light fixtures is moonlight.

As a group of ten we make our way to the dining room, passing the large upholstered chairs, the receiving room with the gold-leaf ceiling, the table covered with the lace-trimmed runner, silver tray placed carefully upon it, silver water flask and cups just so, and the bathroom with a little round window in the door that makes it look like a ship. A little farther down we pass the big door that is always locked because there's a safe inside.

Grandma walks with straight posture. She calls it carriage. I think she's beautiful.

The dining room is very fancy. The silk wall coverings, drapes, and chair seats have a fruit-and-flower design. The silver chandeliers sparkle and the marble fireplace has logs piled high. The mahogany table is fully extended and covered with a pressed white tablecloth and napkins monogrammed with a capital C.

Sometimes our relatives in Duluth come to visit Grandma when we are here. Many others live far away but Grandma tells us about them. My brothers and sisters and I listen carefully because Mom and Dad never tell stories.

Grandma has seven grandchildren in our family and six in the Johnson family. Our family has Thanksgiving with Grandma and the Johnson family has Christmas. We visit at different times during the year, never together. I think it's because the mahogany table isn't big enough.

Steve pulls out Grandma's chair. Mom, Dad, and my brothers and sisters and I look on.

"Thank you," Grandma says.

We wait behind our chairs until she is seated and comfortable.

Grandma always sits at the head of the table and she smiles at everyone. Steve gently pushes her chair in and we all take our seats. I sit next to Grandma, on her right. She strokes the back of my hand.

The large napkin is soft and smooth and it hangs past the sides of my legs. It's like a large tablecloth for my dolls, and it's big enough for magic tricks. This morning I watched Hazel press the napkins and the tablecloth with the big mangle downstairs in the laundry room. Steam came rushing out the little holes as the big roller did its job.

Caroline and Frieda are dressed in their black evening uniforms. Frieda let me see the lace up close one time and I touched the tiny design that felt like soft loops.

As the presentation plates are silently taken away and the formal dinner plates are placed in front of us, I imagine the maids are ladies in waiting for Grandma. Individual silver and blue salt-and-pepper shakers stand like soldiers at twelve o'clock, right above each dinner plate. The light shines in colors through the crystal glasses. The silver chandelier, light fixtures, andirons, and silver trays sparkle. Grandma has taught me the names of the silver and shown me the curly monograms.

"My father especially liked fish and strawberry shortcake," Grandma says. "He liked to read the cookbooks."

I can almost picture Great-grandfather Chester, Great-grandmother Clara, and the entire Congdon family sitting at the table.

A purple-and-yellow pansy floats in the water of the crystal finger bowl that sits on top of a delicate lace doily. I rinse my fingertips, one hand at a time, and I dry them with the large napkin just like Grandma showed me.

She smiles and nods. I know that I have done it just right. But even if I made a mistake she would never be mad.

It's the middle of the night at our house in Minneapolis. All of a sudden the light in my bedroom is so bright that I squint and cover my eyes with the back of my hands.

I open my eyes. Mom is standing with her back facing me. She's still dressed in the navy blue shift that she was wearing when I went to bed. She keeps slamming the lid of the antique box that hangs on the wall. It holds the ribbons for my ponytail.

"Why aren't these ironed?" Mom screams. She's facing me now and her thick hands are on her hips.

"I don't know," I whisper. I try to sit up but I'm trembling so hard that I fall back. I quickly roll out of bed before she comes and drags me out. I just know something bad is going to happen.

"Get downstairs and iron them!" Mom yells. "Now!"

Silently, I pick up the rainbow of ribbons.

Mom shoves me as I walk through the door. I almost trip and fall but I don't dare drop the hair ribbons.

I creep down the stairs in the dark, fumbling for the banister.

Mom storms off to her bedroom.

I run my fingertips along the cool wall in the laundry room. I feel for the light switch and then I flip it on. The overhead light shines on the ironing board. The water level of the steam iron is halfway to the top of the little glass tube. The two prongs of the electric cord fit perfectly in the outlet near the floor.

I tap the metal plate of the General Electric Steam and Dry iron to feel for heat. There's a chill in the air. Standing on one foot I curl the bare toes of my opposite foot to keep them warm. Just like Hester, our housekeeper, I place a thin white cloth over the ribbons that look like silk so I don't ruin the delicate material. I iron back and forth, back and forth until the ribbons are perfectly pressed. I carefully inspect each one before I unplug the iron and wrap the long cord around the metal base.

The laundry room light flickers.

Our black lab runs into the room. Her toenails make a sound like a piano timer on the blue-and-white linoleum floor. Delilah blinks her eyes like she just woke up.

I grasp her red leather collar before I flip off the overhead light. Then together we climb the stairway in the dark of night.

Once a week Mom goes to the Looking Glass beauty salon at Dayton's department store. Large crystal chandeliers look like icicles. All the ladies are dressed in pink and Mom sits in a pink chair when she has cream rubbed on her face. She gets her hair washed and trimmed by a lady with a pink apron and she sits under a dryer that looks like a pink astronaut's hat. Mom soaks her feet in water with pink bubbles and she eats lunch while another lady gives her a pedicure.

"Haircut with Theresa, for my daughter," Mom says. "Facial, manicure, and pedicure for me, with Ramona."

The lady behind the counter opens a big pink book and she runs her finger down the page. It takes her a minute to find the appointments.

"Yes, here we are," she says.

Like magic, a lady appears and she takes Mom with her.

"Stay here," Mom says without looking back. "Theresa will come for you."

The lady behind the pink desk is busy helping someone else. Ladies with little hats and big purses check in for their appointments.

I stand perfectly still, trying to be as good as I can while I wait.

"Suzanne, I'm Theresa," a tall, skinny lady says. She has curly dark hair and a little pink barrette. I don't say a word as I follow her down the pink hallway to a little room with a door like an accordion.

Theresa hands me a pink-and-white-striped robe to wear over my dress. It's like a kid's bathrobe with little ties around the waist. It looks like the puckered material that Mom calls seersucker.

I sit on the pink chair with the extra cushion. I peek at my yellow dress beneath one of the front flaps of the robe.

Theresa squirts water on my hair with a little plastic bottle. The water drips down my neck.

I shrug my shoulders so I won't get wet. I thought I was supposed to get a shampoo.

The scissors make a crisp snap as pieces of dark brown hair fall in my lap. Theresa cuts faster and faster. Soon my shoulder length hair will all be cut off. I'm sure this is a mistake.

"No, just trimmed!" I say.

"Your mother said a pixie cut."

"No, I don't want it!"

Theresa stops cutting and puts the scissors in her pocket. Without saying another word she grabs the tan plastic handle and opens the accordion door. Then she leaves the room. Soon she comes back with Mom who has cream on her face.

"You're having a pixie. Not another word!" Mom screams. "You don't keep the hair ribbons pressed!"

I forgot to iron the ribbons one time. Just once.

Mom storms out to have the cream washed off her face by another lady in pink.

A tear trickles down my cheek. I quickly wipe it away.

Theresa keeps snipping my hair. I want to tell her that I try to be good but I don't know the rules because they always change.

When I get home I run to the plywood tree house, which is cradled among three large oak trees in our backyard. The thick rope burns my hands as I scramble over the large knots and skin my knees on the bark. I claw my way to the top level and shut the trap door behind me. But even the second floor of the tree house isn't high enough any more.

I worry that I will be like the little girl named Sara Crewe in *A Little Princess*. She has to live in the attic because people are mean to her and there isn't any more money.

I am desperate to be a Girl Scout but Mom says, "No." She won't let me have friends and I'm not allowed to play with kids outside of school. Last week, in secret, I made a pink ribbon sash with pretend badges for courage, art, reading, hiking, and nature. One by one I pasted them on the shiny pink ribbon.

I race down the path at Brule with tree roots and pine needles beneath my feet, leaving a trail of sunflower seeds and raisins in the forests of pine, fir, and birch. I can find my way with a compass but I leave clues in the woods to be sure.

The birds are singing to each other and I smell the fresh, clean air. The branches of the trees creak in the breeze.

I stop and spread my arms out wide and embrace the trunk of the largest tree as I lean my face against the bark. My fingers do not touch and I wonder how big the unseen gap truly is but I stretch a little farther so the big tree knows it's a hug.

Great-grandfather's Duluth pack has green fabric and brown leather straps that hang over my shoulders. I pull out the satiny pink ribbon sash. It sparkles in the sunlight that peeks through the forest. The round paper badges are decorated with brightly colored crayon designs. As I slide the sash crossways over my shoulder, I imagine a canoeing badge for a warrior princess.

Grandma has told me stories about the Indians. "Canoes were made from different trees: birch, spruce, cedar, elm, and hickory," she said. "Birch was the fastest and easiest to turn." Grandma used to sit high on the stern deck of the green wooden canoe so she could see as she paddled down the rapids. Her initials, EMC, are painted on all the canoes in the boathouse and they're burned on the blade of each paddle so we can find them if the canoe tips.

Grandma says the woods are heaven because they are so beautiful. I think God lives in the woods, near the trees and flowers and lakes and rivers. Grandma said that God would save the footprints we left in the sand when I told her I wanted to take them home with me. Sometimes on Sunday, the wooden pews are placed outside for church at Iron River. I think God likes the quiet so He can listen. I know that God hears my prayers because He always brings me to Grandma.

CHAPTER IV

BRILLIANT EVENING STAR

When I approach a child, he inspires in me two sentiments;
tenderness for what he is, and respect for what he may become.
— Louis Pasteur

Grandma holds my hand tightly as we walk along the L-shaped pier. The gulls flap their wings and hover before they soar and simply disappear, only to turn up a few seconds later. Their outstretched wings have white feathers edged in black. When they land it looks like they have little gray capes and pink stockings as if they are dressed to greet us.

The dark green metal on the pier is cold and wet. It's where the boats used to be tied up so they wouldn't float away.

"Mooring bollards," Grandma says.

The cool breeze blows my short hair. Grandma's perm stays curly and neat.

As we turn back towards Glensheen we see Pete and Andy helping Bob plant flowers in the garden.

We wave and they wave back.

The square brick-and-stucco boathouse has eighteen tiny curved steps. Grandma said she counted every one.

"Where do the steps go?" I ask.

"The top of the boathouse," Grandma says.

"Can I see it?"

Grandma nods. "We can go look," she says.

The steps are small and narrow with cracks in the stucco. The wall made of stone feels cool as I brace myself on the way up. Grandma is close behind.

The flat cement roof has brown weeds growing in the cracks. It smells like old grass. The railing that goes all the way around looks like milk bottles made of cement. Lake Superior goes on and on.

A ship sails by in the distance. *"William A. Irvin,"* Grandma says as she points to the rust-colored freighter.

"What did you do up here?" I ask.

"My family had parties and dances. La Brosse orchestra played beautiful music," Grandma says. "You could hear it throughout the property."

"Were you in a long dress?" I ask.

"Oh, yes," Grandma says. She holds out her hands and I put mine in hers. She starts to dance and I follow, smiling and giggling. "All the ladies carried little dance cards," she says.

"What for?" I ask.

"To keep track of their dancing partners," Grandma says. "I think I still have some."

Grandma goes first as we make our way down the tiny steps that curve around the edge of the boathouse.

"Forget-me-knots," Grandma says. She points to the tiny baby blue flowers with yellow centers on the other side of the little gravel path between the boathouse and the pier. The little flowers sway in the breeze. "Let's sit by the lake and I'll tell you a story."

"Okay," I say.

The small granite bench is perfect for two.

"Do you remember when I told you about the *Hesperia* yacht?"

"At Brule. You said a yacht is a boat."

"The *Hesperia* was named after my mother, Clara," Grandma says. "It's her middle name."

"Clara Hesperia Bannister," I say. "She's a Congdon, too."

"That's right," Grandma says.

"What does Hesperia mean?"

"Evening Star," Grandma says.

"Who picked it?" I ask. "I mean, the name of the yacht."

"My father did." Grandma puts her shoulders back and she sits tall on the granite bench. She still has strong arms even though she doesn't canoe or row the boats anymore.

"What does Clara mean?" I ask.

Grandma thinks for a minute. "In Latin it means brilliant or clear."

"Brilliant evening star," I say.

Grandma's eyes twinkle. "That's exactly what it means!" she says.

"What did the yacht look like?"

"The *Hesperia* was wood, painted white, with her name in black."

"Did the yacht go in the boathouse?"

"She did, and her special flag was taken down and folded beside her. It was a swallowtail," Grandma says. She uses her finger to draw a shape like a triangle on the palm of her hand.

I lean over so I can see up close.

"The flag was dark blue with a white star. A smaller white swallowtail was inside the blue one and it had a blue C," she says. "Can you guess what that stands for?"

"Congdon!"

"Yes, very good."

"That's my middle name," I say.

"Yes, it is."

"Can I see the yacht?"

The little collar of Grandma's dress flutters in the breeze. Her pearl earrings match her necklace. "Just a picture," she says. "The *Hesperia* caught fire in 1916, many years ago when she was being refueled. No one was hurt but there was too much damage to repair."

"Did you bury her in Lake Superior?"

"No, but that's a good idea," Grandma says. "My father and his friend, Mr. Heermans, owned another yacht called *Sea Wolf*."

"Where is it?" I ask.

"The yacht stayed at the Olympia Boat Club in Washington."

"Grandma, can you tell me another story?" I ask. Her face glows in the sunlight.

"A long time ago, there was a big black ship called the *Salt Lake City*," she says. "Some businessmen gave it a new name, *Chester A. Congdon,* to honor my father."

"Great-grandfather Chester?" I ask.

"Yes, indeed. The ship was well over five hundred feet long. Like the freighter you see in the lake right now."

The long black-and-white ship sailing in the distance has big black smokestacks.

"One night in 1918, the ship was filled with Canadian wheat. Big crested rollers were very tall and dangerous." Grandma rocks back and forth and she moves her hands up and down like big waves. "The storm caused the ship to toss and turn and it hit big rocks. Everyone on board was rescued. No one was hurt."

"Good," I whisper.

"The ship later broke in two during another wild storm, and it sank."

"In Lake Superior?" I ask. "In this big lake?"

"Yes, near Isle Royale, a beautiful park and forested area," Grandma says. "Many boats and ships sank in Lake Superior."

"*Titanic?*" I ask.

"Good guess, but not the *Titanic*," Grandma says. "The *America, Cumberland, Emperor,* and the *John Jacob Astor.*"

"Do you think they crashed because there weren't enough stars?"

"I don't know," Grandma says.

"I bet Great-grandmother Clara's evening star could have helped," I say.

"I think you're right," Grandma says.

The breeze off the lake picks up and the waves have little white crests. Small white flowers, like bells, line the path by the little green shelter where we have picnics. "Lily of the Valley," Grandma says as we head back to the house. "They grow from a little bulb. Then they spread."

We walk on the stepping stones by the formal gardens and pass the dolphin fountain. A little balcony looks over Lake Superior.

The screen door squeaks as Grandma turns the small doorknob. The big door behind it is open so the fresh lake breeze can fill the house.

"Wait for me in the library, please," Grandma says. "I'll be right back." After a few minutes I hear the rustle of her dress as she comes down the hallway.

Grandma opens her hand, like a surprise. It's a dance card with a capital C on the front!

I trace the letter with my fingertip. "It's an Old English C," Grandma says. White silk threads connect the card to a little white pencil. Inside the card there's a thin piece of paper like a fairy wing.

"Sixteen lines for the names of dance partners," Grandma says.

I count each one.

"You may have this," Grandma says. "Please keep it safe."

"I will," I say. "Thank you, Grandma."

I keep the dance card hidden among the pages of my white leather Bible at home in Minneapolis. Sometimes I pretend that I am dancing. My Madame Alexander dolls never tell.

"I would like to take you to a very special place," Grandma says to my brothers and me.

"Okay, Grandma," Pete says with a grin. He runs his fingers over the top of his head. "It's a butch haircut."

"Very nice," Grandma says.

Andy's glasses are thick. "Mr. Magoo," Pete teases.

Grandma leans forward and she speaks into the intercom near the doorway of the study at Glensheen. "James, could you bring the car around, please?" She hangs up the old-fashioned black earpiece, and then she picks up her short white gloves and black leather purse with the brass snap.

We all walk to the front door, staying close by her side.

"Mail isn't here yet, Grandma," Andy says. His fingers sweep across the table in the vestibule.

"A little early," Grandma says.

James is waiting at the front door. His gray suit is freshly pressed. His black shoes are shiny like mirrors.

"Good morning, James," Grandma says. "Forest Hill, please."

James grasps the silver handle on the back door of the emerald Cadillac. Pete climbs in first and slides along the back seat. Andy kneels on the seat and looks out the back window as he shimmies closer to Pete. Grandma waits to be in the middle. I climb in last.

Tiny raised seams cover the back of Grandma's gloves like rows of seeds planted in the garden. I touch one and follow it all the way to the thirteen silhouettes of grandchildren on her gold charm bracelet.

James takes one more look in the rearview mirror. The little button in the top of his chauffeur cap is surrounded by eight triangles of gray material like pieces of pie. His cap matches his suit perfectly. He drives slowly along London Road past Crystal's pink grocery store and Henry's Hamburgers. Last year we asked Grandma if we could try the fifteen-cent burgers. They were juicy and good. Grandma stood in line, too.

James turns right and takes the steep hill that he calls trouble in winter. But it's summer now. The trees are full and green once we get to Woodlawn Road. The neighborhood is like a beautiful forest. After a few minutes James turns right at the driveway to Forest Hill Cemetery.

"This is a beautiful place," Grandma says. "Very special." Red and yellow flowers with bright green stems line the entrance. The window of the Cadillac is cracked open. The air smells like perfume.

Grandma has often told us about this place but we have never seen it. The road seems to go higher and higher. "Is this a mountain?" I ask. "A little hill," Grandma says.

The gravestones and statues get bigger and bigger the closer we get.

James stops the car and steps out. He opens the back door and stands like a soldier at attention.

I climb out and watch as he holds out his hand for Grandma. She places her white-gloved hand in his. Then she steps onto the gravel road.

Andy steps on the footrest and jumps out. Pete waits his turn. Then he bends his knees and takes a flying jump with his arms stretched in front of him.

"Now see here," Grandma says. She never yells but Pete knows that he shouldn't fool around.

Together we walk toward a tall cross. Grandma stops, closes her eyes, and takes a deep breath.

"Very peaceful here," she says. "The Congdon family plot." There's a fancy design on the big cross.

Pete and Andy run around to the back.

"Celtic cross," Grandma says. "Made of granite, a special type of rock. The four arms of the cross stand for water, fire, earth, and air."

Pete and Andy step back to see how tall the cross is.

"The patterns have special meanings. Immortality and eternity."

"Forever and ever, Grandma?" I ask.

"Yes, forever and ever," Grandma says. She points to the headstones for Great-grandfather Chester and Great-grandmother Clara; they're closest to the big cross.

Pete and Andy crouch down so they can look at the initials, C.A.C. and C.B.C.

"Where's baby John?" I ask.

"Oh, of course," Grandma says. She takes a few steps to the left. "He's right here. You remembered him. That's very nice."

I lean over to touch the headstone. Grandma places her soft hand over mine and we feel the cool granite together.

"Do you miss him, Grandma?" I ask.

"I never met him because I was born later. I think about him, though. I'm glad he's here with everyone."

"With his family," I say.

"Yes," Grandma says. "I'll be buried here someday, too. You can visit if you like."

"I will, Grandma," I say. "I will come." A patchwork quilt of green grass and gray headstones covers the family.

"My brother Walter's grave," Grandma says. She points to the headstone.

"They had to cut off his foot," I say.

"Yes, he was a young mining engineer," Grandma says. "He stumbled and his foot was run over by an ore car." She takes a step back. "Walter's wife, Jessie Hartley Congdon, and their first child, Chester Adgate Congdon, the Second."

"Great-grandfather's name," I say. My finger just fits inside the engraving.

"He held little Chester, his first grandchild. It was very special," Grandma says.

"You held me," I say.

"That's right," Grandma says.

We move to the next headstone.

"My brother Ned's grave."

"He took pictures," I say.

"Yes, he did," Grandma says. "Do you remember the darkroom in his bedroom?"

I nod. "Where's Robert?" I ask.

"Someday my youngest brother will be buried here, too."

"What about Aunt Helen and Aunt Marjorie?" I ask.

"My sisters will be very close," Grandma says. "Buried with their husbands' families. Right next to our plot."

"Like next door," I say.

The stone markers are chiseled with the names Dudley and d'Autremont. Pete and Andy walk by each headstone and clear the leaves so they can read the names.

"Is everybody happy here, Grandma?" I ask.

"I truly think so," she says.

The dining room table at home is covered with white feathers, gold lamé, and yards of material in all different colors. It looks like the Dell Fabrics store. Mom is sewing costumes for the third-grade Christmas pageant. The little black sewing machine has a pedal on the floor. Mom guns it just like she does when she drives the car.

The white feathers feel soft as a baby chick.

"Don't touch," Mom says. "You'll get them dirty."

"Are they for the angels?" I ask.

"Yes, but you are Mary," she says.

"Can't I be an angel?"

"No! I told you. You are Mary," Mom snaps. "So forget it." She throws the pinking shears on the table. The jagged ends look like shark teeth.

On the day of the pageant Mom opens a blue-and-white box with a red cross on the front. She pulls out a roll of gauze.

"What's that for?" I ask.

"It's for your head," she says. At Sunday school I have never seen a picture of Mary with bandages. I don't know that part of the story.

Mom wraps the gauze around my head and under my chin, more and more, tighter and tighter. Then she wraps a piece of white wool around my head so it hangs down like a veil. It's hot and scratchy. Mom throws a big piece of material over my head and all of a sudden it's dark. She yanks on the fabric so my head goes through the hole for my neck. Folds of dark blue material fall to the floor. I'm roasting already.

I touch the white veil to make sure it's still in place. I know that I will be in big trouble if it falls off. I can see the other girls with the beautiful angel wings and the sparkly halos made with silver glitter. I'm jealous.

Mom starts wrapping a doll with gauze so it will look like baby Jesus. She says they are swaddling clothes. That sounds tight and uncomfortable.

I feel sorry for baby Jesus. I don't think this is right. It looks strange. Besides it's a girl doll. I want to tell Mom she's making a big mistake but I don't dare. She places the doll in the manger filled with straw. The left arm is high above the doll's head. I wonder if baby Jesus is supposed to wave at the Wise Men.

I walk to the manger, trying not to trip on the ugly dress.

The boy playing Joseph twirls the end of his fake beard. It's held on with a special tape so it won't fall off in the middle of the pageant. He looks at me and points to a little stool.

I tell him that I already know where to sit. Then I take my place next to the wood manger.

The shepherds gather beneath the large yellow star that hangs above the pretend stable. It's dark on the stage. The star isn't lighting the way. The boys wearing the striped head coverings and long robes move closer to baby Jesus. The yellow straw makes a crunching sound. The stable smells stuffy. The Three Kings have sparkly jewels on their hats. They're older boys in the seventh grade. I don't know their names.

I'm not grateful at all to be Mary. I still want to be an angel at the end of the pageant.

"Did we look good?" I ask Mom.

"Take off the dress so it doesn't get dirty!" she yells.

I try to get out of the white veil and the gauze that is wrapped around my head like a mummy, but I can't do it.

"Honey, let me help you," one of the nice mothers says.

"I make her do it herself!" Mom snaps. "She needs to learn."

The nice mother backs away.

My cheeks are fiery hot. I pull the material backwards and somehow the wool veil falls off. The gauze unwraps but it starts to tangle. I get frustrated but I keep trying until I come to the end.

"Fold it neatly!" Mom yells.

All the little girls and their mothers are watching. I can see their red faces and wide eyes. I worry they will think I'm bad because Mom always yells at me. I want to tell them that I try as hard as I can to be good.

It's cold outside the small storefront in Minneapolis. Mr. Andahazy's ballet class has just ended. Thirty minutes go by. Mom never comes to pick me up. I'm afraid it will be dark soon.

In the distance, the green-and-white striped awning of Chrysler's grocery store is flapping in the breeze. I know our house is fifteen blocks from the store because I have counted them, one by one, when Dad drives us home from church.

Neatly shoveled sidewalks are covered with a fine mist of snow that looks like fairy dust. I carefully undo the small silver snap on my pink ballet case, which has a picture of a slim ballerina on the front. At the edge of a little packed snow bank I pull off my white rubber boots and slide my feet into the soft pink ballet shoes with the pink elastic straps that go so nicely over the top of each foot.

I perform an arabesque and then a small pirouette while I hold my rubber boots, one in each hand. The metal zipper of my light blue winter jacket is open.

I skip past Chrysler's Grocery pretending I am the Sugar Plum Fairy in the Nutcracker ballet. Mr. Chrysler comes running to the large picture window and waves at me.

I wave back but I don't stop. I skip and dance down each block. As I reach the white street sign that spells Fremont Avenue I know that I'll be in trouble if I'm not wearing my boots when I walk through the front door of our house.

I brush the glittery snow from the gray calfskin soles as I sit on the neighbor's cold cement steps. The white rubber boots feel heavy on my feet as I walk home in the curtain of twilight.

I'm almost eight years old and I have my own clock. It glows in the dark. The little hand points to the five. The big hand is on the twelve. It's almost time to get up even though it's dark outside. I think of the pink, blue, yellow, and green skating dresses that hang in my closet. They all face forward on wire hangers in case Mom comes to inspect.

Steve is the skating champion but for the past year I have figure skated every day before school, after school, and on Saturdays. It was supposed to be once in a while, as it is for my brothers Pete and Andy. I'm so tired that I can't do my homework and I almost fall asleep in school.

All of a sudden the room is filled with light. I didn't even hear Mom coming. "Get up!" she says.

"I don't want to go," I say quietly.

"You're going!" Mom screams. "Don't talk back to me."

I throw off the warm bed covers and put my feet on the cold floor. After Mom leaves I straighten the sheet and blanket and I make sure there are no wrinkles.

My tan tights are twisted as I try to pull them over my ankles. I can barely reach but I zip up the light blue skating dress with the white trim.

"Get your coat on!" Mom yells. "Get out to the car."

It's cold, so cold I can see my breath. The car has been out all night. The hard leather seat crackles. There's a frosted star pattern on the windshield. Steve is in the front seat. He's almost a teenager. Girls think he's very handsome.

Mom is rummaging through the trunk of the car. She hands Steve his skate bag. She throws mine in my lap.

"Put your skates on now!" Mom yells.

The white leather skating boots are stiff as bricks. The blades are ice cold and sharp like knives. It's a long way to the rink.

I sit in the back seat, watching and waiting.

Steve puts his foot in the black leather skate and starts lacing it up. I wonder if his skates are as cold as mine. I don't understand why we can't let them warm up.

My legs are shaking. I wish I had a thick pair of socks but I know I wouldn't be able to get the Riedell skates on my feet because they're custom made to fit snugly over my tights.

"Get your skates on now!" Mom yells. "I want you to be first on the ice." She looks back and sees that my toes are barely inside the white leather boot. "Do I have to stop the car and put the skates on you?" she screams. She isn't watching the road.

"No, I'll do it," I say. My eyes fill with tears. My right foot is all the way in the skating boot and I lace it up. It's freezing cold. I hold the left skate and try to blow on it. It doesn't help. By the time both skates are laced up, my feet are completely numb.

I touch the soft lining of my white rubber snow boots, trying to feel warm even if I'm not.

"We're almost there," Mom says. "Be sure to get out fast!" Her French roll hairstyle is neatly held together with black bobby pins. I try to count each one to keep my mind off the stinging cold of the skating boots.

The car comes to a stop.

I open the door and step out but my feet are too cold and I fall. I lie in the snow and ice, shivering in the dark parking lot of the Ice Center. Tears freeze on my face.

"Get up!" Mom screams.

"What's going on?" It's my skating teacher's voice. Mr. Lee drove in the parking lot at just the right time.

"My feet," I sob. "I can't walk."

Mr. Lee lifts me with his strong arms as if I'm light as a feather.

Inside the building, I pull on the laces of my skates to get them off. Mr. Lee helps. His face is red as a beet. He doesn't say anything as he wraps my feet in a thick red blanket.

"She needs to get on the ice!" Mom screams.

Mr. Lee walks over to Mom and says, "We need to talk."

Mom throws her hands in the air. She's much shorter than Mr. Lee but her voice is louder.

Steve walks over to the edge of the arena and steps onto the ice. He doesn't say a word.

I think he's very brave.

Mr. Lee comes back and says, "Honey, stay here and warm up. When you're ready, come find me."

After a while I slide my feet into the leather skating boots and tighten the thick white laces until they feel snug.

The new school, Northrop Collegiate, is only for girls. I don't know why. Breck has boys and girls and we all got along. In kindergarten we got to hold the fluffy yellow chicks from Mrs. Andrews' farm. My second and third grade teachers are sisters. Their last names are different because they both got married. I know the names of all the people in the office. Mr. Verbruggen, the gym teacher, has a whistle and he taught us to do sit-ups and push-ups and he showed us how to walk quietly in a straight line. Mrs. Arenz says that I'm so good in math that I could be a mathematician. I love Breck but Dad says the school is too far away.

My navy blue uniform has a V shape in front so the light blue short-sleeved shirt shows through. The navy blue knee-highs itch and the special black-tie shoes are ugly. Even so, I hope that I look like the other girls in fourth grade.

"We're here," Mom says. I barely close the car door. She drives off without saying a word.

The large brick building has cement steps and a long black metal railing. Some of the girls are holding hands with their mothers. I can almost feel Grandma's hand as I walk through the front door of the school.

"I'm in fourth grade," I say to the lady in the front office. I wonder if she thinks that I don't have a mother.

"Down the hall, take the stairs to the second floor," she says. "Mrs. Johnson's room is on the left."

"Thank you," I say, almost in a whisper.

Mrs. Johnson's name is printed on a white index card that is taped to the bubble glass of the classroom door. The room has three long rows of desks and lots of windows. Many girls dressed in blue. No one says a word to me. The desks have masking tape in the corner with each girl's name printed in black. Buffy, Felicity, Bonnie, Jennifer, Linda, Anne.

I've never heard of some of these names. As I look for my own name, I think of my friends at Breck. Veronica, Susan, Beth, Patty, Charlotte, and Laurel, who liked to be called Teenie. I say some of the boys' names to myself as I look for my desk. Evan, Glen, and Bobbie. I wish they were here.

This school is different and the room is old. It smells like varnish. Water trickles through the metal pipes in the wall. My desk is halfway down the middle row. It has a wood flip-top. The desks at Breck were flat like a table because we had cubbyholes in the wall.

I slide into the chair that is connected to the desk. I wonder if they don't want you to run away.

A bell rings in the hallway. It startles me.

"Please take your seats," Mrs. Johnson says. She pulls down a map that covers the blackboard like a big window shade. I have seen maps but I haven't learned geography. At Breck that class starts in fifth grade. I'm not sure if the other girls already know this subject.

"Suzanne, please come up and point to Illinois," Mrs. Johnson says.

My skin tingles. The room spins around me. I shuffle to the front of the classroom, past more desks and more girls than I have ever seen. All the lines on the map look the same. I know the blue is water but I don't know any of the states.

No one laughs or says a word.

Seconds tick by.

I blink and a tear trickles down my cheek. Everything is blurry.

"Anna, can you show Suzanne where Illinois is on the map?" Mrs. Johnson says.

A blonde girl walks to the front of the room and stands right beside me. She knows just where to point on the map.

I feel like I will fail.

In the library at Glensheen the old globe spins beneath Grandma's fingertips. "When I was a girl we learned about places in the world with an atlas, a book of maps," she says. "Or a globe, just like this one."

Her lips curve into a smile and I start to laugh. Grandma always makes it fun.

"The Great Lakes," Grandma says. She points to each one. "If you can remember the word HOMES, you can remember the lakes: H for Huron, O for Ontario, M for Michigan, E for Erie and..."

"S for Superior!" I say.

"That's right," she says. "Good job!"

Grandma draws an imaginary line from Minnesota to New York, then to Arizona, back to Minnesota, and then Wisconsin. She explains each trip with a story. "The Brule River is forty-four miles long and it empties into Lake Superior," she says. Then she traces the route to Washington, D.C. I know that President John F. Kennedy lives there. "In 1908, my father had lunch with President Theodore Roosevelt in the White House," Grandma says.

"Wow," I say. "What did they talk about?"

"President Roosevelt wanted a man named William Howard Taft to be the next president. My father knew other men in politics in Minnesota."

"Did he win?"

"Yes, he did. He was the Secretary of War under President Roosevelt and then he was elected President of the United States."

"President Roosevelt was called Teddy," I say. "He liked birds and forests."

"That's right," Grandma says. "He felt it was very important to protect the great outdoors. He wanted everyone to enjoy the beauty of nature."

Grandma points to the Atlantic Ocean and traces the route to Europe. "It was called the Continent back then. We sailed on ships but now we have planes, too."

"When did you first go on a plane?" I ask.

"In 1932," Grandma says. She holds her arms straight out to the side and pretends she is dipping and gliding. "I flew from Tucson to Phoenix and back. A few months later, a lady pilot flew across the Atlantic Ocean in a big red plane. All by herself."

"Who?" I ask.

"Amelia Earhart," Grandma says.

"Did she wear goggles?"

"She did. And she called her plane the *Little Red Bus*."

I laugh. "I like that name."

"Amelia Earhart did other things, too. She knew that she could do whatever she set her mind to. She wasn't afraid to try new things."

"Was she brave?" I ask.

"Yes, she was very brave," Grandma says. "She flew her plane to many places a long ways away."

"I'm going to Africa someday," I say. "And lots of other places, too."

"That's wonderful!" Grandma says. "Travel teaches us about other people and the world."

"Where did you go?" I say. "I mean, on trips."

"Europe, Africa, the Orient, Jamaica, Bermuda, Mexico, Canada," Grandma says as she traces the routes. "Many places."

I think she must be an explorer because she likes adventure.

Grandma flips through the photo album with the pictures pasted on black paper. "Here it is," she says. She finds the picture she wants and turns the album so we can look at the photo together.

"My father in Egypt," she says. "In front of the temple of Horus on the west bank of the Nile River." Great-grandfather is touching a statue of a bird. "Horus was the Egyptian god who looked like a falcon." Grandma beams and flips to another black-and-white photo.

"That's you, Grandma," I say. She's sitting sidesaddle on a camel that is decorated with large tassels.

"Yes, in Egypt. In front of the pyramids and the Sphinx," she says. "Many years after my father's trip."

I look closely at the picture. Lots of sand and big rocks piled on top of each other. The camel's mouth is wide open like he's yawning. Grandma's dress is covered with a dark coat and she's wearing her white gloves. She has a big purse in her hand.

"You look really pretty, Grandma," I say.

"Why, thank you," she says. She blinks both eyes at the same time, like a double wink.

CHAPTER V

FEAR OF THE UNKNOWN

Deep in their roots all flowers keep the light.
—Theodore Roethke

Summer, 1964

The windows in the living room are wide open but there's not much of a breeze. Pete and Andy are jumping on the trampoline in our backyard in Minneapolis. The coil springs make a squeaking sound with each bounce.

"Grandma is sick," Mom says as she runs up the stairs to the second floor.

"Grandma?" I say. "Where is she?" I twirl my hair around my finger and I hold it tight as I run after her.

"In the hospital," she says. "A stroke. Blood clot in her brain."

"What does that do?" I ask, suddenly afraid.

"She can't talk. Needs a wheelchair," Mom says. "Now don't bother me."

I am nine years old but I don't understand and no one else is around to ask. I don't know what to do, so I pull out my stationery and I write Grandma a letter. *I love you. I hope you feel better soon.* I run my tongue across the back of the stamp and taste the bitter glue.

The blue metal mailbox is one block away. I run as fast as I can. Then I stand on my tiptoes, as I watch the yellow envelope disappear into the mail slot.

I try not to cry but it's hard. Every night I say a prayer: *Please God, help Grandma. Please bring me to her.*

God hears my prayers.

Grandma is resting on the soft yellow sofa in the library at Glensheen. Her dress has pretty blue flowers and a light blue belt.

My four brothers and sisters and I surround her, trying to be quiet.

"I'm sorry you're sick," I say. My voice shakes and there's a lump in my throat.

Grandma holds up her left hand and shakes her wrist so the gold charm bracelet jingles. She remembers! One by one we each find our charm and give her a kiss on the cheek. I want to shrink down and fit in the gold silhouette so I can be with Grandma everywhere, close to her heart. I want to take care of her but I don't know how.

"My name is Mrs. Ethan," the nurse says. There are round-the-clock nurses, one for every eight-hour shift so Grandma is safe. This lady is tall like a watchtower. Her teeth click as she talks. Her hair is brown and curly. There's a silver pin on her uniform. It's a watch and it's right over her heart. The lady smells like lily of the valley, the little white flower with the bells that Grandma called the sweet smell of spring. Grandma follows Mrs. Ethan and me with her eyes.

"Grandma was a nurse," I say. "During the big war, the first one. She rolled bandages and she wore a uniform with a white veil down to her shoulders." I run my hands over my hair, trying to show her.

Mrs. Ethan bends down so I can see her face up close. Her eyes are sparkly brown and she wears bright red lipstick.

"And you know what else?" I say.

"What's that?" Mrs. Ethan says.

"Miss Rosenberry and Mrs. Thorpe were her teachers. I'm gonna be a nurse, too," I say.

"How nice," Mrs. Ethan says.

Grandma chuckles.

I lean over to give her a kiss on the other cheek.

Mrs. Ethan shows Pete how to lock the wheels on the metal wheelchair. "So it doesn't roll away," she says. Steve and Dad help Grandma stand and pivot and Mrs. Ethan cradles Grandma's right arm. She hands me a beautiful white lace pillow that used to be on Grandma's bed. It's made with some of the lace that Great-grandmother Clara collected from all over the world.

I run my fingers over the delicate pattern. Valenciennes lace. Grandma told me. I slide the soft pillow underneath Grandma's right arm. "Good, Grandma?" I ask. "Yes," she says. I see that she can smile on only one side but I know it's still a smile. Grandma can't tell stories anymore but I know the words. I can tell our stories.

There's a new lady at Glensheen. Her name is Vera Dunbar. She was hired by the trustees to be Grandma's personal assistant. Before her stroke, Grandma ran the house by herself.

Mrs. Dunbar is wiry thin with gray hair cut very short. No makeup. She wears the colors of a Northern Wheatear: brown, buff, and gray. Her voice crackles and whistles as she flutters about, just like the bird

Grandma and I saw on the terrace last year. Mrs. Dunbar never touches Grandma's wheelchair. I wonder if she's afraid.

The maids ignore the new lady. They love Grandma and they know their jobs.

Grandma watches it all and smiles. She looks beautiful with her perfect permanent, polished nails, pretty dress, and matching shoes. She still wears her gold watch, gold charm bracelet, and her sapphire and diamond ring. I can almost feel the pearls of her necklace between my fingers.

In the back hallway there's an elevator that's been put in since Grandma's stroke. The elevator is very small but Mrs. Ethan squeezes me in and we stand guard beside Grandma. The elevator jolts and shakes as it climbs to the third floor where she does physical therapy.

I hold my breath until the door opens. I can see the pretend walk way and the little blue wood steps that are covered with black rubber so Grandma won't slip and fall when she does her exercises. I grab the tall handrails as if I'm a gymnast warming them up for her. A thick white belt fits around Grandma's waist for support. Mrs. Ethan holds it snugly as Grandma stands.

I glance at Grandma's shoes to make sure they have a good grip. She moves one foot at a time. Her paralyzed right arm hangs at her side.

I run over and hold her hand in mine. "Good job, Grandma," I say, as she struggles to walk along the little black mat. "Really good." I don't know if she'll ever be able to walk alone but I think she's very brave. "I'm proud of you, Grandma." She smiles as she moves her hand along the silver bar. "This is kinda like gym class," I say. "Yes," Grandma says. She stops and laughs.

When I get home I think about Grandma a lot, hoping she's okay. In the corner of our yard there's a big tree that almost touches the sky. It's so big around that I can crawl past the long branches that hang to the ground. I sit with my back against the large trunk and I read *Nancy Drew*. Nobody even notices that I'm gone unless I do something wrong.

Our house is like a busy train station. People come and go. The milkman in sparkling white delivers large metal cans of milk for our Norris milk machine. The tall man in Chrysler's dark green truck delivers our groceries directly from the store. Mr. Apple owns Apple Pharmacy and he delivers prescriptions in his blue Ford. Sometimes Dr. Lyzenga makes house calls. My sister Becky has her own taxi driver named Happy. He picks her up every day to go skating at the Ice Center. Hester cleans the house, she does the laundry, and she cooks dinner. Her wavy gray hair is covered with a delicate hairnet and black bobby pins. By the afternoon her ankles are swollen from being on her feet all day. She's a great-grandmother. Sometimes her daughter Myrtle comes instead. Sometimes it's her granddaughter, Debbie, who brings her little sister Sigrid or her cousin Carmella.

Pete and his friends watch out for Hester. They grab the large wicker laundry baskets filled with freshly pressed clothes and they run up and down the stairs from the basement to the third floor.

"We'll take 'em Hester," they say. "Don't worry."

"Nice boys," Hester says.

At night I unwrap the forbidden candy. It's the only thing that makes me feel better when I'm not with Grandma. Sometimes it's M&M's, sometimes it's a Hershey Bar or Milky Way, and sometimes it's all three. The crinkled wrappers slide down the back of the walnut headboard in my bedroom. There are so many blue-and-cream-colored drapes on the canopy bed that I'm sure the wrappers will stay hidden.

My sisters are slim. Mr. Lee, my skating coach, says that I'm athletic. I think that I look like the other ten-year-old girls.

But Mom says, "You're too heavy. You need to lose weight so you look better in your skating outfits."

For the first time I wonder if I'm fat even though Dr. Sterrie says that I'm healthy. My Barbie doll is tall and thin and she wears a black-and-white-striped strapless bathing suit. She has blue eye shadow and thick black eyeliner. I don't look like Barbie. She has a ponytail of golden hair and black plastic high heels. Even though I take off her shoes she still stands on her tiptoes when she canoes and hikes in the woods. I wonder if she tries to listen carefully so she can run fast if there is trouble.

"You're going on a diet," Mom says. "Cottage cheese and bananas."

I eat the bananas. Not the cottage cheese. It's white and lumpy and smells like rotten eggs. I hide candy in my desk at school because I'm afraid of being hungry but the hunger never goes away.

I grow a little taller and I sneak into Mom and Dad's bathroom to weigh myself. The needle still points at 76 pounds, same as before. I know that I will never look like Barbie but I don't care. I want to be like Nancy Drew, the girl detective who is smart and figures things out.

Mom measures my waist and hips over and over. She sews more and more skating dresses in blue, yellow, white, and purple. The short skirts never twirl because Mom says she doesn't want to draw attention to my size. Some dresses have ruffles around the neck. One has a monogram in the front. Another has a pleat in the back. I have counted fifteen skating dresses hanging in my closet.

After school I race up the stairs to my room so I can change my clothes. The hardwood floor is bare except for the oriental rug just inside the bedroom door.

I wonder if that's where I will sleep.

My Madame Alexander dolls look straight ahead.

I run clammy palms along the sides of my school uniform, trying to wipe away the shame in my hips and thighs.

"Your mother gave your bed away," Hester says. She can't even look at me.

"Was it the candy wrappers?" I ask.

Hester shrugs. "There's a small bed somewhere. I'll have your brother bring it down."

I wonder how much thinner I have to be. Somehow I know it will never be enough.

"I don't want to skate anymore," I tell Mom. I remember how she yelled when I tried to quit last year but I can't do it anymore. I never liked figure skating and I'm so tired that I'm getting behind in school. I'm nothing like the girls at Northrup. The smart girls have last names that match the department stores, mills, banks, and businesses in Minneapolis. The girls are nice to me but I know I'm different. I'm really one of the poor girls who get bad grades. The teachers are cross because Mom keeps taking me out of school to go figure skating. She says that I have to keep practicing until I do it just right.

I want to study and learn new things so I can be smart. I want to have friends like everybody else. I miss Grandma and I think about her everyday even though we still see her every few months. I feel better when I can hold her hand and tell her how much I love her. I tell our stories and she smiles. I read books to her and she listens. We play Scrabble and Yahtzee. She remembers everything.

"Get your skating dress on *now*!" Mom yells.

"I'm not going anymore," I say. I know this is big trouble but I'm not going.

"I said now!" Mom screams. Her cheeks are fire engine red. Every breath gets louder. I'm afraid of what comes next but I don't care anymore. I want a choice.

I stand my ground and shake my head back and forth.

"Do what I say," Mom screams. She looks like a volcano with red-hot lava erupting from deep inside.

"No," I whisper.

Mom grabs my hair and yanks me off the single bed in my room. I fly through the air and fall with a painful thud on the oriental rug. Trembling, I touch my blistering scalp to see if the hair is still there. It's like the worst sunburn I can imagine.

"You never do anything I want!" Mom yells. "You are the most selfish, stupid, ungrateful daughter. I give you everything."

I cower on the floor.

Mom's thick hands wave in the air as she storms out of the room. There's a whiff of Chanel No. 5 after she leaves.

"Make her skate!" Mom yells at Dad. "I demand it or life will be holy hell." He's been next door in their bedroom the entire time.

Dad slinks around the corner and he stands in the doorway. He doesn't even ask if I'm okay. "If you skate you can have a sewing machine," he says gruffly.

I don't know what he's talking about. I haven't used a sewing machine since seventh grade home economics class when I made the pink dotted swiss nightmare dress that I never wore. Mom takes up the entire dining room table with fabrics and thread, all piled high by her sewing machine. She buys up the entire bolt so no one can have the same material. She constantly winds a thin black-and-white tape measure around me.

"I don't want it," I say. "She pulled me by my hair!"

"This is trouble for me, Suzanne!" Dad says in a loud voice.

Mom slams her bedroom door against the wall.

Dad storms out.

I won't ever skate again.

Fall, 1967

My brown hair is styled in the perfect flip. My bangs are cut straight and the double cowlicks are flattened with hairspray. I am one of fourteen boys and girls dressed in a flowing white choir robe, like the angel costume I never got to wear in the third grade nativity pageant but without the feathered wings or sparkly halo. The starched sleeves are full and drop below my hands. The robe is long, about six inches above the floor, and the purest and most pristine white I have ever seen.

Reverend Norman Lidke, the minister of Hobart United Methodist Church, addresses the congregation. He is a quiet man, tall with dark hair, dressed in a black robe adorned with black velvet trim down the front. "We are here to congratulate these fine young people on their confirmation day," he says.

His assistant is heavyset, perky, and smiling. She practically skips down the aisle with a black plastic tray filled with pink carnations with long green stems. She places the tray on the small oak table at the front of the church. Then she selects a single carnation with a stem so long it looks like a divining rod and she holds it up to the light as if she's blessing the individual petals.

The boy in front of me holds out his hand. The lady whispers, "Not yet." I don't know her name and I bet no one else does either. She picks up a couple of straight pins and the boy realizes that she's going to pin the flower with the long stem directly on his chest. His cheeks are flaming red. Just like the Tower of Pisa he leans way over to the side. He can't get away, though; none of us can.

Eric, the blond-haired boy standing next to me, whispers, "I don't want that sucker pinned on me."

I figure that I didn't study all this time to learn about John Wesley, the founder of Methodism, and memorize the twenty-third Psalm for nothing. But I wonder what it all means and whether I will be different because of the ceremony. I wonder if God will listen to my prayers more closely even though I know that He hears me. He sent me a tutor, Mrs. Specht. She has silvery gray hair and she wears beautiful silk shirts and tailored suits. "You do very well in math and Latin," she told me. I immediately liked her because she had something good to say. When she asked me to tell her a Latin phrase, I said, "Dum spiro spero, while I breathe I hope." Mrs. Specht looked at me for what seemed like an eternity. It was a look of understanding deeper than any words. She knows that what I need is kindness.

I wonder if God will stop the yelling and fighting that goes on in our home because I can pray better or be a better person. When I visit Grandma we go to the copper-topped Methodist church, high on the hill overlooking Lake Superior. Grandma told me about Great-great grandfather Bannister and Great-great grandfather Congdon before she had a stroke. Both of them were Methodist ministers and they had hard times in their lives. I wonder what they would tell me on my confirmation day.

Jonathan, another boy in the class, looks away as the lady pins the pink carnation on his chest. He can hardly keep from laughing. I want to tell him this is serious.

I am next for the holy pinning of the flower and I squirm as the lady pulls the collar of my robe in order to get a better grip. The starched white neckline scratches my fair skin and I sense the hives starting to rise. The lady lets go of my robe and I look to see how far the stem hangs. It's past my hip! The final girl is pinned and the lady smiles like she has just planted the kingdom of heaven on our chests.

The photographer motions for us to squeeze together so he can take our picture. We writhe in agony, knowing the negatives will last into eternity.

The organ music sounds like the song they play in the circus. We parade in single file down the narrow aisle covered with red carpet. No one says a word. By the time we get to the hallway at the back of the small church, Eric and Jonathan have unpinned their carnations. They're fencing with the stems.

Like most Sundays after church, Mom and Dad take my brothers and sisters and me for brunch at the Leamington, a large brick hotel at the intersection of Tenth Street and Third Avenue in downtown Minneapolis. Long buffet tables have white tablecloths that touch the floor and many types of salad, vegetables, and meat. A special table has cakes, pies, and éclairs. I want to taste the chocolate frosting but I'm afraid to reach for a dessert. Mom still watches everything I put into my mouth. Sometimes I don't want to eat at all and other times I sneak down the back stairs to the kitchen and eat leftovers in the dark.

Usually on Sundays we go to a movie that Dad chooses. We have seen *Mary Poppins*, *Doctor Zhivago*, and many scary mysteries. Today I read the words on the marquee: *In Cold Blood* by Truman Capote. I shiver just thinking about it.

"I don't want to go," I say. I'm almost thirteen. My three younger siblings range in age from seven to eleven years old. The youngest has asthma attacks, severe ones when he is stressed. My two older brothers are fourteen and sixteen.

"You're going," Dad says.

Everyone crowds around the concession stand. Mom gets popcorn for herself and then she turns and walks into the theater juggling the red-and-white striped box and her brown leather purse. Boxes of chocolate covered raisins, M&M's, and popcorn are lined up on the counter.

"I don't want anything," I say.

Dad shrugs and walks into the theater with my brothers and sisters.

Reluctantly, I follow. The theater is half full. Tiny lights line the edges of the paisley carpet that covers the aisle. Mom is seated in the fourth row from the front, one plush seat in from the aisle. The rest of us file in. We take up half the row.

The lights are dimmed. Then the theater is completely black.

The movie starts. It's in black and white. A bus is headed to Kansas. Scary men appear out of the darkness. At first I think the farm in the movie is just like Dorothy and Auntie Em's, but each scene becomes darker and scarier.

I pull my navy blue coat over my face.

"Oh, stop it," Dad whispers. He leans over my brothers and yanks the coat from my clenched hands.

The red EXIT sign in the corner of the theater glows in the dark. No one says a word as I get up. The smell of buttered popcorn makes me queasy as I walk up the carpeted aisle and head to the lobby. I take my time looking at the concession stand, the ushers, and the ticket lady. I want them to ask me why I'm watching such a horrible movie but they don't, so I sit in the lobby knowing that I will have to go back in eventually.

I take a deep breath before I head back into the theater. Even though it's dark I can see the outline of Dad's head in the distance, next to the row of children. Mom is between my sisters. I walk heel-to-toe, hoping I have missed the scary parts. The music is heavy and loud. I feel like I'm being trailed but I don't look back.

One of my sisters is asleep in the aisle seat. Mom is the next seat in. I have to step over both of them. Mom sighs heavily, heaves her popcorn box to the side, and pushes me out of the way so she can see. "Move," she says. On the other side of her my youngest sister is also asleep. Thank heavens. My brothers are farther down the row but I don't know if they're asleep or awake.

All of a sudden I see a man on the movie screen with a thick rope around his neck. I think the movie is over, but it isn't. A dark hood covers the man's face. He falls and hangs by his neck.

Finally, the movie theater lights come on. I want to get out of the theater as fast as I can but I look at my little sister Heather and remember when she was left at Uncle John's Pancake House and how the police stayed with her until Dad noticed she wasn't with us. He turned and drove back to pick her up. The policemen didn't say much.

I don't want my little brothers and sisters left in the theater. I count heads. Everyone is here.

Dad is behind the wheel of the station wagon with the wood trim. He doesn't say a word. Mom stares out the window. My brothers and sisters are quiet the entire ride home.

I can't sleep for weeks. I keep thinking of that man hanging by his neck.

Fall, 1967

The beautiful doll with the pointed gold hat and glittering costume stays inside a special glass box on the bookshelf in my bedroom. She was a birthday present from Grandma.

From my bedroom window I see large white clouds that look like clusters of cotton balls in the bright blue sky. The neighborhood is filled with large oak trees and houses connected by sprawling backyards.

But wait, dusty smoke is coming from the tiny window at the top of the garage! My heart pounds against my chest.

Last summer there were two fires, back-to-back, in the kitchen. A fireman wearing a black hat and a long yellow jacket like a raincoat ran up the stairs of our house with a gray fabric hose slung over his shoulder.

The neighborhood kids gawked at the gray smoke billowing from under the gray shingles. The Werler brothers stood on the other side of the street with their mouths wide open. Their parents strained their necks and shaded their eyes from the sun. Everyone was squinting, trying to see what was going on.

Our back Lab, Delilah, sniffed the air. She sneezed from the smoke. Mom sat on the cement steps leading to the sidewalk. She read a book and didn't look up. Dad paced back and forth with his hands in his pockets without saying a word. The blue chalk outline for hopscotch faded beneath his shoes.

The firemen stood on tall metal ladders and sprayed high and low until the trail of gray smoke slowly disappeared. Mom had kept saying that she wanted the kitchen remodeled but Dad had always said no. After the fires, the kitchen was completely redone with a grill and new appliances.

I race to Mom and Dad's bedroom. Mom is reading in bed, eating a chocolate chip cookie. The covers are pulled up to her chest but I can see the top of her white nightgown.

"There's smoke!" I yell. "Coming from the garage."

"Don't bother me," Mom yells back. She sighs and doesn't look up.

"You need to call the fire station!" I say.

"Go away," Mom screams.

I run downstairs taking two steps at a time, grabbing the banister as I slip on the runners. When I reach the hardwood floor at the bottom of the stairs, I fall and scrape my knee but I scramble to the kitchen.

Hester speaks loudly into the phone. "Fire! 4705 Fremont. Please, come quickly."

Dad has just gotten home from work. His face is pale. Rings of sweat drench the armpits of his white cotton shirt as he races through the back door. "There's a car in the garage and there's smoke!" he yells. He gasps for breath as he grabs the keys on the dining room table. Then he races out.

Yellow and orange flames lick the gray shingles on the garage. I can hear the engine of Mom's car. The tires screech as Dad shifts the gray

Porsche in reverse. Tire marks darken the driveway. The smell of melting rubber permeates the air.

Two fire trucks barrel down the street with sirens blaring. The firemen jump out of the red truck with the tall ladder and they race to the garage, fire hose in hand. The firemen spray water high and low, just like they did when the house was on fire last year. They keep at it until the flames are completely snuffed out.

Mom never comes out of her bedroom.

The walls of the garage are charred and leaning outwards, surrounded by black ash and trails of smoke. Particles float in the air. My eyes tear and burn.

The firemen wind up two long gray hoses and load them on the back of the red fire truck. Before they drive away, the fire chief talks to dad for a minute but I can't hear what he says. Dad nods and walks to the back door of the house.

The neighbors head home.

"I want a new garage," Mom says as Dad and my brothers and sisters and I walk through the back door.

"Why weren't you worried?" I ask.

Mom slams her book on the kitchen counter and storms off. She's still wearing a white nightgown even though it's early afternoon.

I frantically search the kitchen drawers. A large box is filled with wooden matches with red tips. I haven't seen it before. The box seems full but there's a white line on the rough black strip on the side. Someone has used at least one of the matches.

I cringe.

I grab the box, open it, and run water over the red tips. I'm queasy as I search high and low throughout the rest of the house. There are no more matches that I can find. I don't know what else to do. Something is very wrong and no one is doing anything about it.

CHAPTER VI

TROPHY CHILD

When I bestride him, I soar, I am a hawk…
—William Shakespeare, *Henry* V, III, vii

Fall, 1969

The rollers of Lake Superior slide over the cobblestone beach as I read Grandma my list of famous people and the names of their horses: Alexander the Great and Bucephalus; Napolean Bonaparte and Marengo; Andrew Jackson and Truxton; George Washington and Nelson; Paul Revere and Brown Betty; King Arthur and Spumador Larmi; Teddy Roosevelt and Manitou; Annie Oakley and Target; The Lone Ranger and Silver; Tonto and Scout; Roy Rogers and Trigger; Dale Evans and Buttermilk; The Cisco Kid and Diablo; Helen Congdon and Dexter; Chester Congdon and Sangamo, Dick, and Harry.

"Yes, yes," Grandma says. She still loves horses.

When Grandma was twelve years old, she rode to town alone on a horse and she belonged to the East End Riding Club that was formed by Mrs. Merrill. She rode to dinner on group dates and then they all rode home again. Julia and Caroline Marshall, Grandma's longtime friends, rode ponies with thick pads and tandem harnesses and they did tricks and jumped over fences in the field. Grandma told me about J.C. Buck, the man from Springfield, Illinois, who bred and owned two famous Morgan stallions, Sentiment and Allen Franklin. Great-grandfather Chester had a particular interest in those horses. Grandma's former suitor, Fred Wolvin, had a Morgan horse named Tanner and he drove him in the ice races in Duluth. Special horseshoes gripped the ice.

"Again," Grandma says.

We both laugh as I read the names again.

It's been less than a year since I started riding. It was supposed to be once in a while but then Mom started buying horses and expensive saddles and bridles. Becky and I were the only ones who had ever taken a lesson but Becky fell off and hurt her tailbone. She never rode again. The only thing Mom used to care about was figure skating until Steve quit. Now I ride every day.

Mrs. Steiner, the hunt master of the Long Lake Hounds, is striking in full hunt attire. Her short gray hair is topped with a black velvet hard hat. Polished black boots, white breeches, scarlet hunt coat, canary vest, and white stock tie complete the stunning outfit. It's a great honor to be invited to ride with her although I worry about the fox. I remember the one that Mom used to wear around her neck. The chestnut-colored fur, the amber glass eyes. When I was a little girl I used to wonder how it jumped up on her shoulders.

"It's a drag hunt," Mrs. Steiner says. "No fox. Wonderful hounds."

The hunt country has beautiful green grass, natural post-and-rail fences, and weathered coops. There's no pressure to win trophies but I feel guilty because all I want is to go to college and become a nurse. I don't know how and I don't know when but I know that someday it will happen.

"You're going to train with Hans Senn," Mom says as we drive home from the stable one evening. I know that he's the famous horse trainer at Helvetia Stable but I like it at Jonathan Stable and I have friends there.

"Don't I have a choice?" I ask.

Mom slaps my face so hard that I see flashing white lights in front of my eyes. For a second I'm unsure if it's actually car lights that are coming at us because we're in an accident. Then I realize I wasn't watching Mom close enough. I didn't see this coming.

Pain spreads across my face like an electrical current with the highest voltage. I can taste the thick blood down the back of my throat.

Blood drips down my face onto my lap. I use my sleeve to stop the bleeding that is coming from both nostrils.

I draw on every ounce of courage that I can muster and with my hands protecting my face I shout, "Don't *ever* hit me again! I will ride with Hans Senn but *do not* touch me."

"You do what I say!" Mom screams.

I see blinking red lights. I can hear the train coming. The whistle blows, short continuous sounds. Wheels grate along the metal tracks. The white crossing starts to come down. Mom leans forward as she grips the steering wheel. She guns the accelerator and races across the tracks.

My heart is racing so fast I can barely breathe. I grab the sides of the brown leather seat but I lose my grip because of the blood on my hands. I gasp as the car sways from the power of the train that rushes behind us. Trembling, I turn and look. The bumper of the Porsche is mere feet from the train that is now racing down the tracks.

I don't know whether to feel grateful that I am alive, deathly afraid of what will come next, or both.

Trembling, I make a silent bargain with God. *Please keep me safe. I promise that I will do something good with my life. Just give me a chance.*

I learn to ride better after working with the famous Swiss trainer and I start winning championship ribbons and many shiny trophies. But I feel the great misfortune that no one understands. The mounting expectations and the guilt that accompanies the excess that surrounds me: custom made Dehner riding boots, coats, breeches, Hermès saddles. All anyone ever sees is the gilded mask that covers a reality beyond comprehension. No one has a clue.

It seems like everything was given to my oldest brother, the former figure skater, and now to me. Mom has had a special shelf made all around the ceiling of my bedroom so the polished trophies can be on display. The ribbons are neatly arranged on a wire hung beneath the shelf. Multicolored championship ribbons with rosettes in the middle, then the blue, red, yellow, white, and pink ribbons. Mom brings people into my room to see the ostentatious display that defines her dreams, not mine. No matter how well I do, it's never enough. "You're only as good as your last blue ribbon," Mom tells me.

Mid-October, 1970

My four brothers and sisters and I are dressed in our Sunday best on a Saturday. Dad is dressed in a dark business suit. Mom isn't home.

We pile into the light blue Buick and Dad drives us to the intersection of Fiftieth and France, about five minutes from our house. He parks the car in front of PETERSON PHOTO. I don't understand. "What's the picture for?" I ask. "Be quiet," Dad says. I pull away as he tries to hold my hand.

It's been about two weeks since the photo session. I haven't seen Dad for at least a week and I suspect that he's gone permanently.

"Suzanne, come down here!" It's Dad's deep voice.

I creep down the stairs of our house in Minneapolis.

The white Dutch door with the hand-painted flowers is open. Dad places one foot in the doorway but he doesn't step any further. His dark wool overcoat, dark suit, white shirt, dark tie, and shiny black wing tip shoes mean business. Short black hair is neatly trimmed. Dark-rimmed glasses frame his pale face and clenched jaw. Large hands sink deep in his pockets.

"I'm leaving," he says abruptly. He quickly pivots and walks down the back steps. The vent of his coat flies open in the breeze.

"On my birthday?" I say quietly. I'm sixteen today.

"I'm leaving," Dad says again. Doesn't even look back. Almost runs to his car, opens the door, and drives off.

"He froze the money!" Mom barks. She brushes me aside as she races past.

"Dad has an apartment," Pete says. "In Minneapolis."

"For how long?" I ask.

"Don't know."

I worry we'll lose our home. I worry about my younger brothers and sisters. I worry that Mom will go deeper into the craziness that I don't understand. I wonder how we will ever get through this.

"He'll be back," Mom shouts as she storms upstairs.

Miss Gray, the principal of Northrup Collegiate, is a heavyset woman with short white hair and audible breathing. She tells me in staccato, "Your father...sent a letter...no longer...responsible...for you or your sisters...I know...this is a difficult time."

I hang my head in shame. Our family is in trouble.

When I get home from school Hester hands me a letter. "From your father," she says.

"He can't give it to me himself?" I ask.

"Don't know," Hester says.

My little sister brings me her letter. We compare. Same words. Dad says he loves us but the words feel wooden and hollow.

"Why didn't he tell us?" she asks.

"I don't know," I say.

I wait until my sister leaves before I rip the letter in half, in fourths, and then in shreds.

The cement-and-glass Hennepin County Courthouse is in down-town Minneapolis. I stand before the judge dressed in my navy blue upper school uniform with the navy silk tie and light blue long-sleeved shirt. My brothers and sisters are frightened and confused. My little sister's lower lip is trembling.

Dad stands off to one side. Doesn't say a word.

"Your father cannot afford to take any of you," the judge says. He fumbles through a myriad of papers.

Dad simply looks straight ahead.

The gold belt buckle monogrammed with his initials, RWL, and the alligator belt and matching wallet, the Triumph sports car that he drove when I was a little girl, all flash before me. Dad recently took my brothers on a cruise to Alaska. He's staying at a hotel. He wears fancy clothes and shoes. Grandma offered to pay for him to go to business school or law school but he said, "No." I heard it myself.

I remember all the checks that my brothers and sisters and I signed at Christmas and our birthdays. All the white cash register receipts Dad saved when we went out to eat or to the movies. I always wondered why. He paid cash, never used a credit card.

The courtroom is spinning around me.

Mom said Dad wants all the money he ever spent on us. He wants the divorce records sealed. The word *sealed* goes over and over in my mind. What doesn't he want us to know?

"I worry there won't be enough money," I say to the judge.

"There's more than enough," he says without looking up. He glances at his watch. It's just one more divorce proceeding taking up his day.

"What will happen?" I ask.

"Custody will be awarded to your mother."

It's not long before my siblings and I each receive another letter from Dad. He's in Germany. *The brioche are good. I'm having a great time.*

I turn on the faucet and watch as the words slide off the page and run down the drain.

It's 2:00 a.m. My brothers and sisters and I now live with Mom in a townhouse in Bloomington, a wooded Minneapolis suburb. Mom's bedroom suite is right next to Rick's small bedroom. My bedroom is down the hall and around the corner, beyond the bedrooms of my two younger sisters. My door is open.

I slowly open my eyes because I think I hear a voice.

"Mom...Mom...I can't...breathe." It's my little brother's desperate cry for help.

I leap out of bed and tear down the hall.

But something is moving in the dark.

I try to make it out. Mom's light is on. As I turn the corner of the hallway I see her shadow looming large as she closes her bedroom door.

Rick gasps and calls for help again.

I race into my little brother's bedroom and feel along the wall for the switch plate. Then I quickly turn on the light.

He's ashen, hunched over, wheezing and gasping with pursed lips.

"It's okay," I say. I grab the green plastic mask and connect the long tubing to the dark green oxygen tank in the corner of his room. I turn the crank and rush to place the mask over his nose and mouth.

Rick tries to adjust the green elastic straps but he's too oxygen deprived. He gasps again.

The door of the mini-refrigerator sticks. I yank on it until it opens and then I grab the bottle of epinephrine that sits on the top shelf. Sterile syringes and needles are piled on the oak table by the wall.

Rick knows that I've never given an injection but I saw it done at the emergency room when he had a severe attack a few weeks ago. "I can do it," I say. Just like the emergency room nurses, I rip open one of the alcohol wipes and clean the rubber stopper of the medication bottle. I check and recheck the dose and I quickly draw the clear fluid into the syringe. Then I tap the side so the bubbles move towards the top and I push the air out of the syringe.

"Just...jam it...in," Rick says, gasping and wheezing.

Slowly, I inject the medication. Then, together, we watch and wait. It takes a minute but Rick starts to breathe more easily. There's a bit of color in his cheeks. Within five minutes he's not wheezing anymore.

"Feel better?" I ask. Beads of sweat cover my forehead.

"I'm okay," Rick says. "Just needed the medication and oxygen."

He drifts off to sleep. His chest rises and falls.

I never tell Rick about Mom ignoring him. But I call his doctor and leave a message. He never returns the call.

Boxes from M.J. Knoud, the high-end equestrian store in Manhattan, start showing up. There are several riding coats in each of the carefully packed shipments. Each one of the coats is neatly folded and wrapped in tissue paper but there are no tags. They must be custom made but the coats don't fit anyone. They look way too small for Mom but she keeps ordering more. Within two months there are well over 150 tailored riding coats in the basement closet. I know they will never be worn.

Meanwhile, Mom disappears for days at a time.

I call Knoud's and they confirm that the coats are custom made by Mom's verbal report of measurements.

Whose measurements, I wonder? "Can the coats be returned?" I ask.

"No, they cannot be returned."

June, 1971

I scan the library as I wait for Grandma and her nurse. The mahogany shelves contain more than a thousand books, many with critiques by Great-grandfather. The textile-covered walls, alabaster sidelights, the ceiling of anaglypta, and the oil portraits of Great-grandfather Chester and Great-grandmother Clara each have a story to tell. The beautiful oil reproduction that Clara painted of Ruben's *King David* is over the mantel. Two silver lamps, from a mosque in Cairo, illuminate the painting. Grecian urns stand like honor guards.

A framed black-and-white photo is sitting on the mantel. I haven't seen it before but something is eerily familiar. I step forward and look. It's the photo that Dad commissioned two weeks before he left home. A family photo sent by the man who left the family.

I turn away and head to the oak-paneled hallway. The rail moldings have picture-hanging cords and rail hooks that support a watercolor with many trees and a long dirt road. Grandma and I used to look at the painting and pretend we were taking a trip together in the great outdoors: Muir Woods, British Columbia, the Alps, and other beautiful places. Now I don't know where the road is taking me. I have absolutely no idea.

As I step through the doorway of the study I sense that something is different. I scan the room. The headshot of Dad is gone. It has already been taken down from the brown grosgrain ribbon that held it alongside the brick fireplace. Dad's picture was on one side and Uncle Chuck's picture was on the other.

Grandma has taken care of it. I realize that she displays the family photo on the mantel of the library because she loves my brothers and sisters and me. It has nothing to do with Dad.

I can hear the afternoon nurse chatting with Grandma as she pushes her wheelchair down the hallway. I hurry so I can meet them halfway. Grandma looks beautiful in a yellow-and-white Liberty print dress and brown leather dress shoes.

"You look lovely," I say.

Grandma lifts her left arm and reaches for me.

I kiss her soft cheek and hold her close. Ever since her stroke I have always read to her when I visit. It's one of our most cherished activities. As I was growing up I read *Harold and the Purple Crayon, Madeline, Little Women,* and *Nancy Drew.* Grandma loved them all. Then I started to read poetry written by her favorite authors: Yeats, Wordsworth, Frost, Dickinson, Austen, Cummings, Whitman, and many others.

Grandma glances at the book next to my brown suede purse. The left side of her mouth curves into a smile.

"I brought one of your favorites," I say. *"Daffodils,* by William Wordsworth." I pull up a chair and open the small book. A gold ribbon marks the page. "I wandered lonely as a cloud that floats high o'er vales and hills..."

"Cloud," Grandma says. She struggles but she says it.

I reach for her left hand. She closes her fingers around mine. "And then my heart with pleasure fills, and dances with the daffodils."

"Yes," Grandma says.

She's never made one complaint since her stroke. Not one. She still travels from Duluth to Brule, Tucson, and Washington. She entertains guests and she sits at the head of the table at lunch and dinner. Last year she came to Minneapolis and we went to the opera, *A Midsummer Night's Dream,* with music written by Benjamin Britten. The pink linen A-line with capped sleeves was my first long dress. Grandma touched the olive green velvet ribbon and the appliquéd flowers on the empire waist. Her own dress was made of beautiful dark green silk.

But I worry about her and all the trials of life that she has had to endure, including the stroke seven years before that resulted in paralysis on her right side and difficulty speaking. And six months ago her eighty-year-old sister-in-law, Dorothy Congdon, shot and killed a seventeen-year-old intruder who broke into her house in Duluth. It was deemed justifiable homicide but it was yet another stressor for Grandma. Dorothy's husband Ned was Grandma's second-oldest brother who died thirty years earlier from a heart attack. Four years before, Grandma's sister Helen died several weeks after an automobile accident. Helen had lost her husband and two of her sons many years before her own death. Grandma's oldest sister, Marjorie, is in her eighties and lives in a house down the road from Glensheen. Her husband Harry died two years ago. One of their sons died when he was only fifteen years old. Three of Grandma's four brothers are gone, too.

As I look at the gilded birdcage in the windowsill of the library, I can almost hear the tiny canary sing and turn its head when the large key is turned. Like Grandma, the little bird is surrounded by splendor but it is never truly free.

After dinner Grandma and I sit on the yellow sofa in front of the crackling fire. My photograph album is filled with over thirty pictures of us at Brule, Tucson, Glensheen, and Great-grandfather's orchards in the Yakima Valley of Washington State. The black cover feels like pebbles beneath my fingers as I place the album on Grandma's lap. She leans forward as I turn to the first page made of black construction paper with individual corner inserts.

In the first photo my long white christening gown is edged in delicate lace that falls beneath Grandma's wrists. Her sister Marjorie, my godmother, stands beside her husband, Uncle Harry.

Grandma smiles and points to the living room around the corner where the baptism took place.

"That's right, Grandma," I say. "I remember the story. It made me feel very special." Grandma sits a little taller in her wheelchair.

In the next photo Great-grandfather's apple and pear orchards seem to go on for miles in the Yakima Valley. Grandma and I stand in front of the trees, both of us smiling. I have an apple in my hand. The large stone house is made of basalt dug from a local quarry.

"I think of our time together whenever I bite into the apples and pears from the orchards," I say.

"Yes," Grandma says. I know the taste of the fruit brings her back, too.

In the background of the next photo there's a large red barn, a big silo, and prize-winning Aberdeen-Angus cattle. My hair is windswept. Four-year-old fingers reach beyond the weathered fence trying to touch the cattle that seem miles away. Grandma stands behind me. She's wearing one of her Liberty print dresses.

Grandma traces my face in the picture. Then she turns to the next page with the photos of us skipping rocks at the edge of Lake Superior, eating a picnic lunch on the beach at Park Point, and both of us walking with Jacques, her gray French poodle after Philippe.

We come to the last photo in the album and I point to the mahogany cabinet with many other albums stacked neatly inside.

"Do you want the ones of you growing up, Grandma?" I ask.

She nods and says, "Yes," very clearly.

I gently place the album in her lap.

She turns to a photo where she is playing field hockey at Dana Hall, the private girl's school in Wellesley, Massachusetts.

"My favorite," I say.

"Ohhhh..." Grandma says. She grasps my hand.

The photo was taken in October of 1909, on a blustery fall day when she was in tenth grade. There was a no-makeup policy and Peter

Thompson uniforms, called "Peter Toms" for short, consisted of a middy blouse, like a sailor shirt with tie, and a skirt with lacing in the back, made of heavy cotton in the spring and fall and navy blue serge in the winter. Girls were required to be outside every day for two hours. Activities included walking, basketball, field hockey, riding, skating, and rowing. Sports, the thinking went, gave young women practical experience in the rules of fair play, cooperative effort, and a sense of honor and loyalty to each other. They learned about fairness, teamwork, and courage.

In the photo, the girls are taking long strides and their hair is blowing in the wind. Grandma is racing toward the goal. That same year she had persistent sciatica and then lameness when she returned home for Christmas. Four months later, in April of 1910, she had back surgery because her symptoms did not resolve. She was hospitalized for almost a month; however, she recovered fully.

Grandma and I look through more photos that capture the active life that she led: canoeing, skating, swimming, snowshoeing, camping, riding, hiking, tennis, fishing, croquet, and sailing. As a young girl she was very involved in physical culture, which included aesthetic dancing and rhythmic and military drills with weighted Indian clubs, bars, and wands. She performed with her gymnastic dancing class at the Lyceum Theater in downtown Duluth. One time she was dressed as an American Beauty rose and another time she was a poppy.

"Grandma, do you remember the golf tournament?" I ask. "You were on the A team."

"Oh...my," she says. "That's...right." She throws her head back and laughs. It sounds like the bubbling rapids at Brule.

Later that night as I climb the stairs, I admire the Tudor Rose design and stylized heraldic shield of the stained glass windows. The same design is repeated on the stenciled walls of the hallway.

Aunt Marjorie's carved mahogany four-poster has a white quilt with royal blue trim folded neatly at the end of the bed. The bed linens are turned down. The delicate white lace canopy and embroidered floral dust ruffle remind me of the canopy bed that I used to have in Minneapolis. Georgian-style highboys stand guard on either side of the Venetian marble fireplace with the sterling silver andirons and tiny acorn design. A lamp with a white paper shade has partially cut-out flowers that bloom like a veritable garden from the heat of the light. White demi-shades cover the light bulbs in the wall sconces. "To protect a lady's delicate eyes," Grandma told me.

The room is warm. The air is fresh even though the windows are closed.

A foghorn sounds in the distance.

After I change into my nightgown I slide into the envelope of crisp white sheets that covers the horsehair mattress beneath me.

Grandma is down the hall. Asleep. Safe.

The night nurse watches over her.

CHAPTER VII

VALOR

When God created the horse, he said to the magnificent
creature: I have made thee as no other…

—The Quran

October, 1973

I try to picture Valor, my thoroughbred horse, as I drive through the wooded neighborhood of Dellwood on my way home from the stable. I imagine my hands over the sides of his face, my cheek next to his. My hand glides down his sleek neck, over muscular haunches, and the large scar that protrudes on his left pastern. His jet-black mane is tousled as he gallops around the paddock like a well-trained athlete. Valor brings me a sense of peace and a connection to my true nature amidst the wild nature of life.

As I pull into the paved driveway of our townhouse I feel a sense of uneasiness. I unlock the front door and take the stairs to the second floor. As I turn the corner in the hallway I can see clothes strewn over the floor of my bedroom.

I race into the room, a disaster zone. My dresser drawers are ransacked. Riding coats, riding boots, dresses, shoes, and blue jeans have been thrown haphazardly on the shiny hardwood floor.

The front door was properly locked, no forced entry. Nothing else that I passed on my way upstairs has been touched.

I tread through the clothing, kicking my own shirts and pants out of the way. My heart is hammering against my chest. The bottom dresser drawer is open. It's empty. My photo album with the pictures of Grandma and me is gone.

This isn't a burglar.

Lightheaded and dizzy, I stumble through the ransacked clothes, search through the closet, every dresser drawer, and under the bed. I don't care about anything but the photo album. But it's not here and I don't know why.

I regain my bearings and head down the hall to Mom's bedroom. She blocks me with her wide stance. Hands on her hips. Dressed in tan breeches, brown field boots, and a starched white shirt, she looks like an enemy commander. Even though she barely rides she still dresses the part every day.

"Where's my photo album?" I demand in a shaky voice.

"I have it!" she shouts. "Riding has to be your complete focus."

A little over a year ago, she wouldn't let me attend my high school graduation because of a conflict with a horse show. "You have to earn points for the year-end championships," she said. When my diploma came in the mail she tore it up. "There's only money for horses not for school," she screamed.

"The album is mine," I say. "Please give it to me."

"You need to focus," Mom says. "The Royal Agricultural Winter Fair is coming up and you need to win points."

The Canadian version of the Madison Square Garden horse show will take place in two weeks. Valor and I have always done well but it's never enough for Mom. Never. No matter how many ribbons or championships we win.

"Please give me the album," I say.

"You heard me!" Mom yells. She shifts from one leg to the other, watching for my reaction. Her face is crimson.

My skin crawls.

"I will ride," I say. "Just give me the album." The album is everything I have of Grandma and me together.

"I'll see in a couple of weeks," Mom says. She storms off, almost smiling.

Nauseated and lightheaded, I turn away. My legs feel weak as I walk down the hall but I steady myself with the second floor metal railing.

I will never be like her.

I will never let her break me.

November, 1973

Two weeks later, I am outfitted in formal equestrian evening dress: black wool swallowtail coat, canary vest, tan breeches, black leather dress boots with a spit shine, brown leather gloves, and black silk top hat.

Valor and I are in perfect form over the working hunter course that simulates the outdoors: white coop, brick wall, green brush, white gate, and post-and-rail fences.

I pace back and forth in the warm-up area as the remaining horses and riders complete the course. Hackney ponies and carriages are lined up for the next class.

It seems like hours as the judges weigh their final decision. I want to tell them what the results mean for me but suddenly my number is called. We've won! Valor and I have won first place in the Working

Hunter Stake class. I breathe in the smell of sawdust and woodchips as I lead my champion thoroughbred into the arena decorated with flowers and international flags.

Prime Minister Trudeau and his daughter, immaculate in their own formal attire, present the silver trophy and first-place ribbon, complete with a brass maple leaf in the center of the rosette.

As I leave the arena Mom grabs the $750 prize check that is stapled to the first place ribbon and she takes off. I struggle to catch up with her as I lead Valor back to his stall.

"Please, can I have the album now?" I ask. "I did what you wanted."

Mom stops and breathes heavily like she does before she yells. Then she wheels, glowering.

I lean back, afraid that she will hit me.

"I burned it," she snaps. "Now forget it."

Stunned, I can't move. I see her distorted image through a pool of tears. It's like a kaleidoscope of brittle shards.

January, 1974

A few months later, I run my fingers down the cloth spine of *Little Women* and flip through the pages. The bookshelf in my room holds the stories that I have loved.

Something falls on the floor.

As I look down I see a couple of black-and-white Polaroid photos. I bend over to pick them up and my knees start to give way. The first one is a picture of Grandma and me. I am six years old, standing in front of the greenhouse at Glensheen holding a rose in one hand and Grandma's hand in the other.

I tremble as I do a double take.

The second photo was taken at Brule in front of the boathouse. A tall paddle dwarfs me as Grandma and I sit on a dark green over-turned canoe. I try to think back. I must have stashed the photos but I can't remember when.

Before her stroke Grandma always carried her Polaroid camera, packets of film, and that pink foam roller filled with developing solution. My brothers and sisters and I surrounded her as we waited for the image to appear.

I snap back to the here and now and I grab my white leather Bible off the shelf. The small envelope with the antique dance card is still hidden between the pages.

It's quiet. No one is around.

I tear down the stairs with the photos and the dance card in my hand. I grab the front doorknob that slips between my fingers. I try again and pull the front door open and then I race to my car parked just outside the garage.

I tear down the road with a stranglehold on the steering wheel.

The green metal of the safety deposit box feels invincible as I place the photos and dance card deep inside.

I will make sure that Mom never finds them.

August, 1974

It's early afternoon at Brule. Ruby-throated hummingbirds surround the tiger lilies and feeders alongside the house. Grandma is resting on the rust-colored sofa on the screened porch that faces the river.

"Canoe," she says. "You."

"Okay, Grandma," I say. "I'll canoe while you take a nap."

Her eyelids are heavy. The sound of the rapids quickly lulls her to sleep.

Velma Pietila, one of Grandma's longtime nurses, twines her arm around mine as we walk the length of the L-shaped porch. Velma's blond hair is streaked with gray and styled in a circular coil like a halo. Large dark glasses frame her face.

"How do you think she's doing?" I ask.

"She tires easily," Velma says. "But she's especially happy when she's here."

"I know how much she loves it," I say. I love it, too. I can almost hear the sound of my fingers, like a card in a bicycle spoke, as I ran them along the smooth wood balusters of the staircase as Grandma and I climbed to the second floor when I was a little girl.

Grandma was in charge of the interior and exterior renovation of the house and property after she purchased it forty years ago. The dining room walls are stenciled with a beautiful Swedish design. The living room has framed Swedish prints on the walls. A small rust and black weaving with an intricate design hangs above the fireplace. It matches the hand-painted design on the ceiling beams. The candlestick holders are fashioned to look like Swedish ladies with long blue dresses, white aprons, and tall candles in their hats. The same design as the bell that Grandma rings in case we need anything at dinner.

As Grandma sleeps I tighten the heavy white straps on the bright orange life jacket and I follow the pine needle path through the woods just as I did as a little girl. I remember how I would collect pieces of birch bark and fold the ends into a long hollow. Pine pitch and Elmer's glue sealed the seam. Grandma and I kneeled as we launched the little vessel and watched it float away.

Today I launch my own solo canoe. The river is the same one that Grandma paddled as she sat high on the stern deck in a simple dress and sensible shoes. The same one that Great-grandfather Chester traversed when he visited friends on the Brule. "The River of Presidents," Grandma said. "Hoover, Coolidge, Cleveland, Grant, and Eisenhower spent time at Cedar Island Estate, the summer White House on the Brule." She met President Coolidge at a party in 1928. She liked his secret service man, Mr. Wood, better than "Silent Cal."

The Bois Brule shoots downward amidst the dense foliage of ash, pine, cedar, spruce, and fir trees that canopy the riverbanks. I challenge the white-crested caps of the rapids as glistening bubbles and feathery foam splash my face. The canoe turns crisply as I paddle, gliding over more rapids and dodging the rocks on the wild waterway.

Quiet water after the riffles mirrors the dense foliage. Trout swim beneath the surface with fins edged in snowy white and blue, and sides of azure dotted with gold, rust, and flecks of scarlet. The water is like a glistening trail behind me, mirroring the blazing cloak of amber and gold that spreads across the sky.

Grandma taught me to be a part of nature, adapting to the environment. I feel as much a part of the solitude and wilderness as the rocks, trees, wildflowers, and flow of the river itself. I inhale the aroma of the wilderness. Mother nature at her finest, the only mother I have ever known.

Grandma's lids flutter and then I see her sparkling brown eyes. She glances at the orange life jacket that I have placed on the wicker chair beside the couch and she smiles. She remembers the sound of a paddle and the feel of it as it moves through the water.

May, 1975

Mom has moved my younger brother and sisters and me to three different houses in less than four years. The most recent one was built at Marine on St. Croix, a city founded as Marine Mills in 1839. It was the site of the first commercial sawmill along the St. Croix River, where there was abundant white pine. Now she's talking about a move to Colorado. I have no idea how she could possibly maintain two homes.

The quarter-mile driveway at the Marine on St. Croix property is steep and partially paved with bricks. I try to contemplate just how many more bricks it will take to complete the expensive driveway. My sisters and brother are standing at the turnaround by the main house. The wooded landscape surrounds them. Becky is eighteen, tall and thin with dark brown hair extending to the middle of her back. She deserves a chance. "I really want to move to Colorado," she says. "And train at the Broadmoor Skating Club."

Heather is petite and thin with shoulder-length brown hair. Angelic face. Almost sixteen. "I'm ready for a change," she says quietly. "I want to go." I want her to be happy but I worry about the effect of the potential move on her and the others.

Rick has a wide smile, round face, and short dark-brown hair. His asthma is well controlled but he's emotionally attached to Mom. I know that I can't change that. He deserves a chance, too. I just don't think it's with the mother he believes in.

I have tried to protect them in the best way I can although I know I wasn't perfect. "You're not my mother," I have heard more than once. Whenever Mom took off for days at a time I felt the weight of responsibility on my shoulders and the burden of guilt for resenting it. But I was the oldest one still at home after Steve left for college, after Pete left to finish school and get a job, after Andy left a few years ago to be on his own. They left, one by one, all within the last five years.

I don't know if I've done enough before I send my brother and sisters out into the world but it's been two years since I completed high school and I feel time ticking away. I made sure that Becky had her driver's license. Soon Heather will be old enough to get her license, too. I know that I can't live in the captivity of Mom anymore. I want a life of my own, yet I wonder if I'm being selfish. I wonder if leaving will mean I have failed my brother and sisters.

Two nights a week I secretly take courses at Lakewood Community College because Mom would never approve. For the first time since third grade I have a transcript with A's in the courses that are prerequisites for nursing school: biology, chemistry, microbiology, and anatomy and physiology.

My shift at Clark's Submarine Sandwiches is from six at night until two in the morning. I earn $1.60 an hour in addition to a second job exercising horses. My black polyester uniform is a dress with a front zipper, orange trim, and matching orange apron. Sometimes I feel like I'm dressed for Halloween. But the trays of ham, salami, turkey, cheese, lettuce, onions, tomatoes, and the smell of fresh rolls for the submarine sandwiches reminds me that I am capable of doing anything if I work hard enough.

As we stand in the turnaround of the dirt driveway that has yet to be paved with bricks, I ask my brother and sisters one more time, "Are you sure you want to move to Colorado with Mom?"

They all nod in agreement.

I scan their faces, trying to take in every feature. "I have to talk to Mom," I say.

The red shingles, white door, and bay window of the guesthouse catch my attention. I know Mom's plan was for me to live there indefinitely, but it wasn't my plan. I've been on the property only once before but I remember the separate building with a garage, three bedrooms, and a large bathroom. It was built for my brother and sisters. Mom wanted the main house to herself.

I knock on the wood door of the house with gray shingles. The smell of fresh paint wafts through the air. I nervously shift from one foot to the other.

I knock again. Harder than before, in case Mom didn't hear me.

No answer.

The brass doorknob is cold even though it's warm outside. The door opens easily with gentle pressure.

Tentatively, I step inside. My hiking boots barely make a sound on the hardwood floor as I walk through the kitchen and living room. A deep red leather chair faces a large brick fireplace filled with logs. Two pewter mugs and a pewter plate adorn the mantel. Antiques fill the dark room. The air feels stale.

"Mom," I call out.

No answer. I wonder if she's trying to hide. Her light gray Audi is parked in front of the house.

I climb the circular wood stairway. "Mom," I say again.

The stairs creak.

I go no further than the top stair. A massive bedroom suite takes up the entire second floor. A large brick fireplace is straight ahead. I scan the room. A king size bed is covered with a handmade quilt. Closets with open sliding doors line the entire wall. At least thirty tailored dresses in a rainbow of colors have price tags still attached to the sleeves.

Mom is sitting in a forest green chair in the corner of the room. She's staring at the page of a book. Can't tell if she's reading or not.

"I've wanted to leave for a long time," I say.

No response.

"I need to live my own life."

"You never do anything I want!" Mom screams. "You are absolutely selfish."

I've heard it so many times before and I won't take it any more. There is nothing to say. I take a deep breath before I turn and walk down the hardwood stairs and out the front door.

March, 1977

The crisp white acceptance letter from the University of Minnesota School of Nursing is the window of opportunity that has opened before me. Grandma is the only person that I want to tell right away.

Caroline, the maid, opens the second set of doors in the vestibule. She embraces me warmly. One time when I was a little girl she invited me to watch the *Lawrence Welk Show* for a few minutes in her tiny room on the second floor of Glensheen. There was dancing and beautiful music.

Vera Dunbar appears from around the corner. "How nice to see you, Suzanne," she says. "Your grandmother is in the library. She's very excited to see you."

"Thank you, Vera," I say. I try to be polite but I can't wait to get to Grandma. In my hand is a small glass vase filled with violets.

The sun is streaming through the windows of the library. Grandma is watching a ship as it sails in the distance on Lake Superior.

"Grandma," I say, as I embrace her. "I love you."

"Ohhh," Grandma says. She touches the tiny violets and smiles. "Love...you," she says.

Velma Pietila greets me warmly. Her white cotton nurse's uniform is neatly pressed, as always.

"Hello, Suzanne," she says.

I give her a hug. "Always nice to see you," I say.

I gaze at the unconventional beauty of Grandma's face, the short gray hair with the perfect perm, the sparkling brown eyes. Her paralyzed right arm is supported with a small pillow covered in lace. I think it reminds her of her mother, Clara.

"Point de Flandres," I say.

"Yes," she says.

Grandma's beautifully manicured nails have the faintest pink polish. A thin brown leather belt matches her tailored sepia wool dress. Sheer nylon stockings and stylish dress shoes complete the perfectly matched outfit. Grandma stands tall despite being confined to a wheelchair. Even though her speech has grown softer and her movements restricted, she never lost a meaningful connection with others. She is determined to stay engaged in a world that means so much to her.

I gently touch her left hand like a piece of prized porcelain, noting the sapphire and diamond ring that she always wears on her little finger. The gold charm bracelet that I know so well is like a garland of grandchildren.

"Grandma, I was accepted into nursing school," I tell her. "I will start this fall."

"Really!" she says. She smiles and gently pulls my hand close to her chest. "I...was...nurse," she struggles to say.

I look deeply into her eyes and tears well up in mine. During World War I she was one of eleven women in the first home nursing and first aid course at St. Luke's Hospital, planned as a reserve force for service in civilian or home nursing. Wearing a veil and uniform, she also completed a surgical dressings course, later rolling regulation bandages for use overseas.

"There were many types of bandages and dressings," Grandma told me. "Gauze sponge, gauze wipe, gauze square. Even bandages with tails for a soldier's head or to hold dressings on the abdomen."

"I remember. I'm so proud of you, Grandma," I say. "I love you."

"Love...you," Grandma says. She points to the study across the hall.

I grab the handles of her wheelchair and Velma Pietila walks alongside. Velma never takes her eyes off Grandma, always making sure that she is safe.

A framed picture of Valor and me sits on Grandma's desk by the window. Velma places the glass vase filled with violets right beside the photo.

Grandma points to the portrait she had commissioned of me as a child. The little girl in the black velvet dress looks back at us.

"I remember her, " I say.

"Me...too," Grandma says.

"You will do well, Suzanne," Velma Pietila tells me.

"Yes," Grandma says. She gently squeezes my hand.

PART II

DARKLING

CHAPTER VIII

DARK NIGHT OF THE SOUL

The grief that does not speak whispers the
o'er-fraught heart and bids it break.
—William Shakespeare, *Macbeth*, IV, iii

June 27, 1977

It's just past sunrise. The muscular chestnut gelding is nipping, pawing at the dirt and shaking his head, uneasy.

I release the snap clamp of the twisted cotton lead rope and watch as he gallops across the grass-lined paddock. Hidden in the dirt, the shallow depression of a killdeer nest has a single blade of grass, a few tiny stones on the periphery, and four small eggs. An adult bird with spindly legs shrieks an alarm call and stiffly moves away from the nest. One wing is hung low and dragging on the ground, feigning injury.

"Call for you!" Myron shouts as loud as he can. "Emergency!" Striped overalls hang on his thin frame like a scarecrow.

I race to the barn. My brown leather paddock boots slip on the dew-covered grass.

Sasha, the stable dog, runs to my side. The Rottweiler thinks it's a game.

Myron's eyes meet mine. "Your sister," he says. "She's on the phone, crying. Just keeps crying."

I don't know if it's Heather or Becky as I run to the indoor arena. My sisters have been back in Minneapolis for almost a year after realizing they could no longer live with Mom in Colorado. Becky is in college and Heather is working full time.

I wrestle with the long phone cord like it's a runaway horse.

"Hello?" I say. I can hear sobs on the other end of the phone but no words. "Heather, is that you?" I ask. "What's wrong?"

"I don't know if I can tell you," she says.

"You can tell me," I say. "What is it?"

"Grandma," Heather says between sobs.

"What about Grandma?"

"She's dead," Heather says.

My legs buckle and I grab the wall, my fingers clawing at the plaster.

"Murdered," Heather says.

I feel the blood drain from my face.

"Mrs. Pietila, too," she says.

"Murdered?" I whisper into the phone. The possibility of Mom being involved is beyond the shadow of a doubt. But I don't say anything. I don't want to upset Heather any more than she is already.

"Pete just called," Heather says. "I think...one of the trustees called him."

"Are you okay?" I ask. I try to stay composed but my voice shakes.

"Don't know," Heather says.

"What happened?"

"One of the brass candlesticks," Heather says. "Second floor hallway."

"What do you mean?" I don't understand what she's trying to say.

"Mrs. Pietila was... bludgeoned."

I gasp. There are no words.

"Still there?" Heather says. "Are you there?"

Finally I get something out. "But Velma retired about a month ago," I say. "Are you sure?"

"She filled in," Heather says. "Another nurse couldn't come."

"And...Grandma?" I say.

No answer.

"What about Grandma?" I ask. My forehead is against the wall.

"She was...smothered," Heather says.

I feel lightheaded. Like I will faint. My heart is echoing in my ears.

"Wasn't she...at Brule?" I ask. Grandma often spends the weekends in Wisconsin during the summer accompanied by one of her nurses.

"She came back last night," Heather says. "Like she always does." "Have you talked to Steve?" I know that he visited Grandma at Brule this past weekend.

"No, but Pete did."

"Has everyone been called?"

"Pete called them," Heather says. "But...I wanted...I wanted to be the one to call you." She knows how much I love Grandma. She loves her, too. We all do.

"Is there anything I can do?" I say. I try to be strong, but my courage is fading.

"No," Heather says. "Nothing."

I take a breath. "Are the trustees making funeral arrangements?" I say, choking up.

"Yes, they'll let us know tomorrow," Heather says. She starts to cry again.

"I love you," I say. "I'll get back to you in a couple of hours."

"Love you, too," she says.

As I hang up all I can think of is that I should have been there. Grandma needed me and I wasn't there. Velma Pietila tried to protect her but she couldn't do it alone. I sweep the tears away and wipe my hands on the smooth leather chaps that cover my jeans. I grope for the edge of a wooden stool as I fall, a feeling of extended slow motion.

Sasha sees me from the aisle in the barn and she comes running. She leans into me, her massive body warm and muscular, her paw on my thigh. I wrap my arms around her neck and bury my face in her thick black fur as I start to sob. She does not move.

"Good girl, Sasha," I whisper.

Myron leads the horses in, one by one, from the paddocks. The sound of heavy stall doors closing, followed by the bolting of metal latches, reminds me of the work that needs to be done.

My legs are wobbly as I stand and brush myself off.

Sasha escorts me down the aisle of the stable. The large Rottweiler protects me. A white star on the left side of her chest doubles as a sheriff's badge. The lights are bright. The aisles are swept clean and the metal carts are filled with sweet alfalfa.

The metal sliding door at the front of the barn is wide open. A curtain of dirt and gravel partially camouflages a gray Jeep Wagoneer coming at lightning speed down the long driveway. The Jeep comes to a grinding halt just outside the stable door.

Hans comes dashing toward me. "What's the name of your grandmother?" he pants.

I shiver. "Elisabeth Congdon," I say. "Did you hear the news?"

"It's on all the radio channels," he says. The top of his head shines in the heat. Gray flecked sideburns are damp with sweat. He fingers the single black pen in his shirt pocket.

"I just heard from Heather," I say.

"Are you okay?" Hans says. "Anything I can do?" He shifts from one foot to the other. His gaze is focused on me.

"No, nothing," I whisper.

All the television channels air pictures of Grandma and Velma Pietila from a few years ago. The reporters are already estimating the value of Grandma's estate to be somewhere between thirty and fifty million dollars. Videos show policemen, detectives, and canine units searching the grounds of Glensheen. Yellow police tape is wound around the black metal gates, cordoning off the estate. News reporters stand by with microphones, anxiously awaiting information.

Grandma was 83 years old. She escaped the scourge of childhood illness at the end of the nineteenth century and beginning of the twentieth: typhoid, tuberculosis, polio, smallpox, scarlet fever, diphtheria, measles, and influenza. She survived a stroke, diabetes, and breast cancer and she outlived her entire family. She was blessed with an inheritance of privilege and now cursed by unimaginable tragedy.

Velma Pietila, the Finnish nurse, was sixty-six years old with forty years of nursing experience. For thirteen years she cared for Grandma. She'd retired to spend more time with her husband and family. But she'd come back one more time, to fill in.

I don't sleep more than an hour at a time. Every sound is magnified tenfold. Every scratch of an animal in the gravel outside my window is someone coming after me. A recurrent dream frightens me as I linger between sleep and wakefulness. It plays over and over in my mind even after I am awake. I see myself in a long white sleeveless gown flowing like chiffon behind me. Over my heart there's a crimson stain. Silently, I run in bare feet down a black asphalt driveway that extends into the eerie night. The driveway is the exact pattern of the one at Glensheen; however, in my dream it is endless. My feet move rapidly but they don't touch the ground. My arms flail as I run faster and faster. My shoulder length brown hair streams behind me in the wind. My face is pale, my hazel eyes, large and wide open, frantic. My lips are parted but I am stone silent.

Grandma wasn't protected. I go over and over it in my mind. I wonder what I should have done. Whether I could have saved them both if I had been there. But all my thoughts and conjured up ideas are shattered to pieces as the profound questions of fate, accident, and intention flash before me.

June 30, 1977

I feel the cool breeze of Lake Superior on my face. I am twenty-two and a half years old, the same age as Grandma when she attended her father's funeral in the mahogany library of Glensheen almost 61 years ago. Great-grandfather Chester had a pulmonary embolism and acute dilatation of the heart. He died on November 21, 1916, in St. Paul, Minnesota. His casket was placed in the private railroad car of John H. McLean, General Superintendent of the Oliver Iron Mining Company, and brought to Duluth. Chester Adgate Congdon was 63 years old.

I wear the dress Grandma loved the most, a tailored dove-gray silk-and-wool blend with three-quarter length sleeves and twenty-four tiny covered buttons symmetrically placed down the back. My small gray leather purse holds the antique dance card and a pressed white cotton handkerchief edged in delicate lace and embroidered with tiny white flowers.

The fresh lake air has floral overtones from the formal gardens. The leaves of the dense trees, surrounding the estate, whisper in the background. My close friend Mary is at my side. Her large body encases a heart as big as all outdoors. Her long dark hair is swept off her face. She's dressed in black and wears no makeup.

Mary takes in the English Tudor design of the carriage house with the diamond paned windows, hipped roof, and side gables. "Is this the house?" she asks.

I shake my head, turn and point to the large Jacobean manor house made of brick and stucco and straight and curved Flemish gables. Multiple chimneys point to the sky.

I search for the window to Grandma's second floor bedroom. A cream-colored window shade is pulled partway down like a flag at half-mast.

Mary follows as I make my way across the asphalt driveway that curves throughout the estate just like the one in my dream. I want to tell her how difficult this will be. How afraid I am that Mom will make trouble. My tears are just below the surface but I hold them in, knowing that if I start to cry I will not stop.

Mary touches my elbow. "I'm right here," she says. She knows what I have been through with Mom because she worked with Hans, the horse trainer, for many years. It's comforting to know that I don't need to repeat the story.

Silently, I head for the shoreline at the edge of the estate. A rust-colored freighter sails in the distance. It's the *William A. Irvin.*

I step out of my gray leather heels and leave them in the freshly mowed grass before I make my way between the cobblestones and scattered driftwood. A small flat rock with smooth sides is right in front of me. I pick it up and I feel Grandma's arms wrap around me. With a flick of my wrist I send the rock skipping three times across the glistening water.

The rocks are cool beneath my feet as I make my way back to the lush green grass. "For Grandma and me," I say.

Mary nods.

One by one, I slide my feet into the gray heels.

I pick a few forget-me-knots just across the narrow gravel path and I cradle the tiny blue flowers with the yellow centers in my hand. Grandma used to tell me how the elegant little blossom was a sign of remembrance, faithfulness, and love.

Mary follows me onto the gravel path that leads to the brick-and-wood shelter. A cluster of lily of the valley is just around the corner. I pick a few and carefully wrap the delicate wildflowers in my lace-trimmed handkerchief and place them in my purse. Then I lead the way over the manicured lawn. The brick path winds through the formal gardens. Glistening lily pads and snowy white blooms float in the pool of the dolphin fountain, made from a single block of white marble. Large goldfish used to swim here when I was a little girl. Grandma gave me rides in a little plastic boat, pulling me around the entire pool.

The long asphalt driveway curves toward the front of the house.

All of a sudden I see a tall, thin stranger with salt-and-pepper hair slicked back from his face. He's wearing a dark suit, white shirt, and dark tie and he's heading toward us, hands deep in his pockets, moving like a missile aiming for a target. I swerve.

He swerves, mirroring me. Very quickly, he's in front of us. He reeks of alcohol. There's a curved cut on his upper lip crusted with dried blood. His face is lined with leathery wrinkles. Dark eyes penetrate mine.

I want to run but I can't. I'm frozen in fear.

"Roger Caldwell," he says in a deep voice. "Here with your mother." He holds out his right hand. His palm is purplish blue and green. His entire hand is swollen.

I turn away but out of the corner of my eye I see someone peering at us from the first floor sewing room. White curtains frame the person's face. I can just make out the short dark hair. I gasp. I'm certain that it's Mom.

I will my legs to move. But the man steps in front of me again and leans toward my face.

"Just trying to make this easier for you," he says in a gruff voice.

I turn my back to him and motion to Mary. We take off running toward the formal gardens, racing to the reflecting pool by the fountain. We stop, both of us breathing heavily.

I glance at my watch. It's forty minutes before the funeral.

"Here he comes," Mary says beneath her breath.

I grab her elbow and we race down the cement footpath, then across the little wooden bridge that leads back to the carriage house.

"Where are you going?" the man yells.

I'm breathless as we reach the carriage house door that is slightly ajar. I glance back over my shoulder just as Mary and I step inside.

The man is still by the main house. He turns and throws his hands in the air.

"Who is he?" Mary says.

"No idea," I say, as I wipe my tears with ice-cold fingertips. "Clearly connected to my mother."

After a few minutes we creep toward the house, pausing to make sure the driveway is clear. We walk toward the white oak front door that will lead the way to where Grandma is waiting. As a lady, she was never late. This time is no exception.

I feel the sweat on my palms and a chill from the lake breeze as Mary and I pass through the arched front doorway of the house. There's a small dark table beneath the Linden glass window in the vestibule. A flat oval plate, made of oak and carved in the pattern of a water lily, is still there. It was the mail drop where Grandma's letters magically disappeared and the day's mail was delivered.

Linden glass doors separate the front entry from the interior of the house. For the first time in my life they are wide open.

Vera Dunbar wrings her hands and paces back and forth. Gray bangs cover her eyebrows but her eyes are red and swollen.

"Oh, Suzanne," she says in a shaky voice as our eyes meet. "Your grandmother loved you...very much." Her face is ashen. She's like a tiny bird, fragile and scared.

I nod. "I loved her, too."

Vera slides her arm around my waist as my eyes fill with tears. I take a deep breath as I try to compose myself.

"I'd like you to meet my dear friend, Mary," I say.

"How nice of you to be here for Suzanne."

Mary nods, not saying a word.

But I'm focused on Vera. "What happened?" I whisper.

"No one knows," she whispers back. "Plain-clothes policemen are stationed throughout the house."

"Who is the man with my mother?" I ask.

"Her new husband," she says. "Roger Caldwell."

"Husband?" I say. I didn't even know that she had remarried.

My gaze follows the fumed white oak paneling accented by the hand-carved pilasters, and up the steep white oak staircase with the balustrade intricately carved to resemble interlaced strap work. The tufted merlot velvet cushion is noticeably absent from the landing bench. I suddenly remember it's where Velma Pietila's body was found. I tremble and look away.

"Where's Grandma?" I ask. "In the library?"

"Yes," Vera says. "People are just starting to go in."

"I need to be with her."

"Of course," Vera says. "I'll walk with you."

I feel her tiny hand on my back. But before I can turn and walk down the hallway, a disheveled heavyset woman with short dark hair and large round glasses races past me. Her funeral attire consists of a tight blue shirt, white stretch pants, and white tennis shoes. She barks incomprehensible orders and gestures wildly to no one in particular, behaving as if she's at a party instead of a funeral.

I back away in horror. I haven't seen her for several years but there is no mistaking her identity. It's Mom.

Vera and I exchange long glances.

Without a word we walk past a blond man in his thirties, wearing a three-piece brown suit and brown tie. His upper body is draped over the top of an oversized upholstered wing chair in the formal entryway. He definitely is not a member of the Congdon family, but I have no idea who he is.

The large entryway to the mahogany library is framed with maroon velvet drapes appliquéd with gold galloon, the same special decorative trim used for ecclesiastical dress and military uniforms. The drapes conceal the pocket doors fused with white oak and mahogany. I used to play hide-and-seek in the luxurious fabric and I used the drapes as stage curtains when I dressed in the antique clothes and put on fashion shows for Grandma and her sisters.

Once inside the library, I gently touch the beautiful mahogany of the casket to let Grandma know that I'm here. The lacquer is so clear I imagine it will ripple if the wind blows.

Large dark ferns with trailing fronds adorn the top of the casket.

"A gift from Bob Wyness," Vera whispers. I know how much Grandma meant to him. Bob's grandfather was the master gardener for a tea merchant in Montrose, Scotland. His father, George, had worked at the Clayton and Eagle Rock estates, owned by Henry Clay Frick. George Wyness was hired away to become the head gardener at Glensheen. Bob followed in his footsteps.

Mary follows as I lead the way to the hardwood chairs beneath the oil portraits of Great-grandfather Chester and Great-grandmother Clara. Portraits of Grandma's maternal great-grandmother and great-grandfather grace the walls by the fireplace. They are watching over her.

The antique globe reminds me of how lost I feel in the Congdon family, my immediate family, and the world.

My brothers and sisters are seated throughout the library. One by one our eyes meet and we nod in quiet acknowledgment. No one says a word.

Mom and the gray-haired man are slouching at the end of the yellow sofa smiling and conversing. Heather is sitting on the sofa, too. Clearly uncomfortable, she pulls closer to Becky.

My six cousins sit in white folding chairs in front of the lakeside windows. The chairs remind me of a wedding, not a funeral. Aunt Jennifer and Uncle Chuck are seated next to their children. The two families fill the library. The tension is palpable.

About a hundred extended Congdon family members, friends, and staff are seated in the formal living room adjoining the library. The velour portieres and over-curtains are appliquéd with gold galloon just like the drapes in the library. Guilford fireside chairs and a large sofa upholstered in tapestry are filled with relatives. The red tones of the Angora damask wall covering are highlighted by deep flame mahogany woodwork. *Waterfall of Mino,* a meticulously embroidered picture in silk, hangs by the terrace doors. Grandma let me stand on a chair when I was little and I looked at the tiny stitches.

A minister from First United Methodist Church officiates. I've never seen him before. He stands beside the Nubian marble fireplace in the living room. As he speaks his first words of address, amplified by a microphone, the hundred people grow still. "On this day of heartfelt sadness we gather to remember Elisabeth Mannering Congdon, our dear one. She was a loyal and generous supporter of the Duluth and Tucson communities, educational institutions in the United States and overseas, and multiple charitable organizations. She tirelessly devoted her time and philanthropic efforts to the arts and charities that supported women and children. Her family, grandchildren, great-grandchildren, friends, community, and all who loved her will miss her deeply."

Muffled voices sing a hymn that I don't recognize. I wonder who chose it. After the final prayer, the minister says, "We will now proceed to the cemetery for the interment."

Steve, Pete, and Andy, wearing neatly pressed dark suits, dark ties, and highly polished black shoes, walk forward and surround Grandma's casket. They join three other pallbearers and together they grasp the brass handles, lift the casket, and step forward in unison. Grandma's spirit and grace fills the hallway as she leaves the family home for the last time.

Mary and I and the others follow.

The pallbearers gently slide the casket into the shiny hearse. The rear door is closed.

"We're all here, Grandma," I whisper.

The first limousine seamlessly links the long row of cars that looks like a string of black pearls. The back door is open. A knot forms in my stomach as the white stretch pants and white tennis shoes come into view. The gray-haired man with the cut lip sits in front of Mom. They're laughing and joking.

My siblings are wedged together in the first row of seats.

I look at Mary and she nods. I know that I have to do the unthinkable. Holding my dress close, I slide along the smooth black leather seat.

The gray-haired man turns around. "Just trying to make this easier," he says with an oily grin. The smell of alcohol makes me nauseous.

The limousine begins to move. Throngs of media people are waiting just outside the wrought-iron fencing that surrounds the estate. They peer into the dark windows, cameras ready.

I close my eyes as the cortège heads toward Woodlawn Avenue. The heavily wooded road is peaceful and for a few minutes there is total silence.

The driver slowly turns into the entrance of Forest Hill Cemetery. He follows the winding road up the hill.

My heart sinks.

Reporters swarm around the family plot.

Policemen hold the crowd back.

The limousine comes to a stop. As I step out there's a stampede to the left. The group dashes to the casket as if they are trying to be first in a race.

The minister is waiting at the graveside. He speaks briefly. All I can do is watch his lips as he mouths the word "Amen."

"Amen," we all say.

My relatives and the others quickly disperse to the waiting limousines and cars. Media people are busy packing up their cameras and video equipment under the watchful eye of the police.

I wait a few minutes until everyone walks away. Then I move slowly toward the grave. I lift the flap of my gray leather purse and gently grasp the beautiful wildflowers wrapped in the white cotton handkerchief. I bend down and release the tiny bouquet with the sweet smell. The flowers free fall, landing in the middle of the ferns on top of the casket that is now deep in the ground.

As I make my final and private tribute, a canopy of dark birds flies overhead.

CHAPTER IX

FAMILY MATTERS

...every unhappy family is unhappy in its own way.
—Leo Tolstoy, *Anna Karenina*

July 6, 1977

It's six days after the funeral and nine days after the homicides. I sit alone at a white laminate counter with gold flecks at Janzen's restaurant in White Bear Lake.

The waitress changes the channel on a black-and-white television set.

"Roger Caldwell was arrested today," the local newscaster says.

I gasp. It's him, the man who accosted Mary and me at the funeral. Mom's new husband is the murderer!

Two men seated at the corner table are deep in conversation. Baseball caps are pulled over their eyes. They don't look up. As I listen to the gruesome details of the news report, I plan my getaway before anyone else comes into the restaurant.

Roger Caldwell was arrested at Methodist Hospital in Minneapolis shortly after midnight for two counts of murder. He was admitted to the hospital yesterday, on the fifth of July, due to loss of consciousness possibly related to drinking while taking Antabuse. Grandma's jewelry and wicker case were found in a hotel room that Roger Caldwell shared with Mom after the homicides. Identified as Marjorie Caldwell, Mom is allegedly involved in the crimes.

Just like I suspected.

The two men sitting at the corner table grab their checks and get up to leave. One looks at the television screen and shakes his head back and forth. The other man strolls to the cash register. A bead of sweat slides down my back. They both listen for a minute before they snuff their cigarettes in the black plastic ashtray at the end of the counter.

I want to run and hide but I stay glued to the red plastic stool as the latest details of the investigation unfold.

Four days earlier Roger and Marjorie Caldwell were seen in Golden, Colorado, at the hotel where they apparently lived. Grandma's 1,700-year-old Byzantine coin was found in their hotel room. It had been stolen from the curio box in her bedroom at the time of the homicides. Roger Caldwell allegedly mailed the coin to himself in an envelope from the Radisson Hotel where he had stayed with Mom at the time of the funeral.

I grab my purse and leave a crumpled dollar bill on the counter.

My hands shake as I grasp the steering wheel of my Pinto, trying with all my might to stay on the winding road.

As I drive onto the stable property I see Hans come running. He meets me at the sliding door completely out of breath. "Your mother's husband," he says, as he gasps. "Arrested!"

"I never put it all together," I say. "Not until now. When I heard about the homicides I initially thought my mother had hired someone." My heart is hammering against my chest. "Possibly someone in organized crime."

Hans nervously shifts from one foot to the other. His forehead is lined with wrinkles. "Why would you think that?" he asks.

"I don't know. The rumors of organized crime in the horse world," I say. My thoughts are jumbled. "I didn't know...I was so confused about it all."

"No criminal organization would be involved," Hans says. "Definitely not with your mother."

I listen to his trusted voice.

"Unfortunately," he says. "This is probably just the start of things to come."

Deep inside I know he's right.

The media coverage of the investigation is continuous. Two weeks after the homicides the lead detective executes a search warrant of Roger Caldwell's safety deposit box. The contents include a power of attorney and a handwritten and notarized will signed by Marjorie Caldwell, leaving 2.5 million dollars of a multi-million dollar inheritance to Roger Caldwell.

Surrounded by the patina of well-oiled saddles and pictures of champion horses, I can't even begin to comprehend what I don't know.

"Call for you," Hans says.

I pick up the phone in the tack room.

"Suzanne LeRoy?" It's a male voice.

"Yes," I say.

"John DeSanto, Assistant District Attorney for St. Louis County, prosecuting the homicide case."

"Whose side are you on?" I ask, tentatively, and other television shows but I'm still confu
helping the wrong people.

"I represent the State," he says. "I'm working Elisabeth Congdon and Velma Pietila." He seems to have picked up on my confusion.

"I want to help," I say. "I think my mother is involved." DeSanto does not respond to my statement. I sense that he cannot. I vaguely remember the newspaper photos; early thirties, medium height, dark hair, tented moustache, thick-rimmed glasses.

"Would you consider speaking to the detectives?" DeSanto asks.

For a second I wonder if I'm in trouble. Then I realize that it's not about me. "Yes," I say.

"Detective Gary Waller will be in contact with you."

The next day the detective calls. He's professional and to the point. "Let's meet at the Ritz-Carlton in Minneapolis next week," he says.

I wonder why we are meeting at such an upscale hotel but I don't ask.

Beneath the crystal chandelier in the bustling Ritz-Carlton lobby there are ladies wearing Chanel suits with gold buttons and fabric flowers. Grandma used to stay in this hotel whenever she visited Minneapolis.

I glance at my neatly pressed tan pants, green knit sweater, and polished loafers. I wonder if I should have dressed more formally.

Two men approach me. One has blond hair and a light brown moustache. He's professionally dressed in a three-piece brown suit, white shirt, and dark brown tie. I immediately recognize him as the man draped over the wing chair on the day of Grandma's funeral.

ʓanne, Detective Gary Waller." He holds out his large hand.

m grip. My palms are clammy. Wonder if he noticed. "My partner,
Detective Dick Yagoda," he says.

Yagoda offers his hand. Firmer grip. He's tall, a little over six feet.
I glance at his dark brown wavy hair and muscular build. Looks like a
football player in a neatly pressed suit.

"Lets head down to the restaurant and get some breakfast," Waller
says. "We can talk there."

In between the two of them it feels like a detective sandwich. I scan
Waller's back looking for the outline of a gun, maybe a shoulder holster
or a pistol in the back of his belt. Not a trace. But there's something
under his arm. Looks like a photo album, but I'm not sure.

The detectives head to a tan vinyl booth in the hotel restaurant.
They don't wait for the hostess.

I slide into the side next to Yagoda, careful to stay a few inches away.
Waller is seated across from us. I wonder if it's protocol. There are a few
customers in the restaurant but no one is even remotely close.

Waller pulls out a small notepad with unlined white pages and black
binding at the top. He grabs a shiny black pen from the chest pocket of
his suit coat.

Meanwhile, a waitress in a light blue uniform and matching apron
brings us a couple of menus. Her curly gray hair is covered with a hairnet
and she has a name badge with printed block letters that spell JULIA.

I wonder how the detectives would sum her up. I wonder if they are
summing me up.

"What'll it be?" the waitress asks.

"Just coffee, please," I say. I want to tell her I'm not the one in trouble. I'm just trying to help. I wonder if she thinks I did something wrong.
I wonder if she has read about the case and the horrible woman who just

happens to be my mother. I look for signals between the waitress and the detectives and I start to worry.

"Same for us," Waller says. "We'll be here awhile."

The waitress nods. She writes the orders on a lined green notepad with a No. 2 pencil. The detectives track her as she walks into the kitchen. Then their attention turns to me.

Waller reaches inside his suit coat and pulls out a small black leather case. He flips it open and flashes a shiny police badge. Just as quickly he puts it away. "Thank you for meeting with us," he says.

I nod. "How did you know it was me?" I ask. "I mean, in the lobby?"

"I saw you at the funeral," Waller says.

"Were you near the oversized wing chair?" I ask. "Just inside the entryway?"

"Yes, I was there."

I look at Yagoda. "Were you there?" He glances at Waller and doesn't say a word.

The waitress appears seemingly out of nowhere. The detectives watch and wait as she sets a gold-colored coffee pot and three white porcelain coffee cups on the table. Then she takes off.

Yagoda pours coffee for all three of us.

"Detective Yagoda and a number of other plainclothes policemen were in the house during the funeral," Waller says.

My face flushes. "You were inside Glensheen the entire time?"

"Yes, during the funeral," Waller says. "We went to Forest Hill Cemetery for the burial and then we returned to Glensheen."

"Where in the house?" I ask. "I mean before the funeral."

"Some of the men were upstairs," Waller says. "Some of us were on the first floor."

"Was Roger Caldwell a suspect at that time?"

"Yes," Waller says. "We were suspicious."

"And you didn't watch him?"

The detectives glance at each other. Yagoda raises his eyebrows. They clearly don't understand where I'm headed.

"I was accosted," I say. "By Roger Caldwell. The day of the funeral."

"I had no idea," Waller says.

No kidding, I think to myself.

"What happened?" Waller asks. He rubs his fingers against the knot in his tie.

Yagoda still hasn't said a word.

"I came with a friend," I say. "Caldwell approached us as we walked up the driveway. He reeked of alcohol and tried to follow as we ran to the carriage house." I shudder just thinking about it.

"Where did he go?" Waller asks.

"He got angry and walked off."

"I didn't know that happened," Waller says in a calm voice. He fingers the edge of his moustache.

I wonder what they were doing. If the two prime suspects weren't being watched, what was going on?

"Can you describe Roger Caldwell?" Waller asks.

"Salt-and-pepper hair, slicked back. He wore a two-piece dark suit. Leathery facial appearance, and there was a cut on his upper lip with crusted dried blood. I thought he'd been in a fight."

"Did he say anything to you?"

"Just his name and that he was with my mother," I say. "He seemed very nervous and his right hand...it was swollen and bruised. I didn't want anything to do with him."

Waller scribbles a few notes.

"There's something else," I say. "I think my mother was watching us from the first-floor sewing room."

Waller stays on topic. "Had you ever met Roger Caldwell before the funeral?"

"Never. I didn't even know that my mother had remarried," I say. "I didn't associate Roger Caldwell with the homicides at the time."

I haven't touched my coffee but Yagoda tops it off. The steam curls into the air.

"When did you last see your mother, Marjorie Caldwell?" Waller asks.

I have to think for a minute. "I believe it was almost two years before the funeral."

"How was your relationship?"

"Terrible."

"Can you elaborate?" Waller asks.

I breathe deeply. "I wanted to leave home for a long time but I stayed because of my younger siblings." I don't want to go through the details but I know I must. "My mother tried to completely control my life," I say. "She opened my mail and listened in during my phone calls."

"Why do you think she did that?" Waller asks.

"To make sure I wasn't planning to leave," I say. I wonder if he thinks I did something wrong but he quickly changes the subject.

"Tell me about her spending habits," Waller says.

"Completely out of control. There were at least a hundred fifty riding coats, all custom-made, but they didn't fit anyone. She simply made up measurements."

Waller nods. "Go on," he says. I wonder how much he already knows.

"She kept buying more and more horses. I asked her to stop but she wouldn't. She even stole from my sister's savings account."

Waller nods and takes a sip of his coffee. He doesn't rush me but the questions keep coming. "Do you still have horses?" he asks.

"One horse named Valor," I say. "I plan to sell him before I start nursing school this fall. The other horses were sold a few years ago. My mother hasn't been to the barn since then."

Waller flips the pages of his notepad but he doesn't write anything down. "How is your relationship with your father?"

The curtains across the room flutter as a waitress races past.

"I haven't seen him since I was sixteen," I say. "When my parents were divorced."

"Why is that?" Waller asks.

The same curtains have a stray thread hanging off to the side. I didn't notice it before.

"I never thought of him as a father. I saw him hit my mother over money issues when I was a little girl," I say. I remember sitting on the floor of my closet with Raggedy Ann. "He never hit me but I didn't trust him. He told my siblings and me to endorse checks that were gifts from my grandmother. I never knew what he did with the checks after that."

"Where did you grow up?" Waller asks.

"In Minneapolis. We lived in a house near Lake Harriet. After the divorce my mother moved us to a double townhouse in Bloomington, not too far away."

The questions keep coming. The detective shows no emotion.

"Were there other homes?" he asks.

I try to recall each one. "A house in Mahtomedi...and there was another one at Marine on St. Croix. The main house burned down shortly after my mother and siblings moved to Colorado."

Waller nods. Nothing seems to faze him.

"According to the newspaper account there were no charges," I say. "Apparently she didn't try to collect insurance."

"The policy had lapsed," Waller says. I sense he is aware of everything. "Any other fires?" he asks.

The waitress walks by. Waller waves her off.

I wait until she is out of earshot. "Two at our Minneapolis home on the same day," I say. "And another fire in the garage about a year later."

Waller flips back through his notes.

"Oh wait, she..." My voice cracks. "She burned my photo album with the pictures of my grandmother and me."

Waller knows to give me a minute.

I take a deep breath but I sense there's something else. "Were there other fires?" I ask.

"There were fires at a bank in Colorado," Waller says. "Two days back-to-back. September of last year."

"Wasn't she charged?"

"Marjorie Caldwell was a suspect because she had created trouble for the bank. She was allegedly seen when fires were set inside but there were no charges."

"She had a volatile relationship with the trust officer in Minneapolis," I say. "I remember her screaming into the phone when she was trying to access more funds."

"Your mother has spent several million dollars over the past eight years."

I gasp like I did in second grade when the wind was knocked out of me in gym class. "Where did she get the money?" I struggle to say.

"She had interest in several trusts and she coerced your grandmother into co-signing several loans over the years. Defaulted on all of them," Waller says. "Well over five hundred thousand dollars."

I lean forward and look the detective in the eye. "Why didn't anyone help my grandmother?"

"The Congdon trustees finally had a conservatorship established by court order."

The word *finally* sticks in my mind. "Who were the conservators?" I ask.

"Vera Dunbar, Dr. Elizabeth Bagley, and William Van Evera, one of the Congdon trustees," Waller says.

"Vera Dunbar?" I say in disbelief. "She's very frail. Dr. Bagley is an older woman, too. I can understand protecting the money but what about protecting my grandmother?"

Waller nods.

Yagoda runs his fingertip around the rim of a white porcelain cup with dried coffee stains on the side.

"Do you have any knowledge of the marmalade incident?" Waller asks.

"I don't know what you mean," I say. I grab the edge of the vinyl seat and brace myself.

"In November of 1974, Elisabeth Congdon became very ill and was unable to be aroused. Marjorie allegedly fed her homemade marmalade."

Suddenly nauseated, I try to comprehend the horrific details.

"Your grandmother's blood tested positive for meprobamate, a drug with significant side effects," Waller says.

"My grandmother wasn't prescribed that medication," I say.

"That's right," Waller says.

I scan the restaurant. Six other customers are seated across the room.

"Wasn't anything done?" I ask. "Charges filed?" My voice is shaking.

"The Congdon family, your relatives, didn't want to investigate," Waller says. "Didn't want the publicity."

"What? You've got to be kidding me," I say. "They didn't protect my grandmother?"

"Didn't want to pursue it," Waller says. He's so calm as he says it. Like it's just another detail in his busy day.

"That's despicable! My grandmother was a vulnerable woman."

"I know this is difficult," Waller says. "Need a minute?"

"No," I say. I take a second to think. "Last week...about two weeks after the funeral, I spoke with Ken Maine of the Congdon Office."

"Why was that?" Waller asks.

"He conveyed his condolences and then we had a serious talk. He told me that the Colorado Bureau of Investigation had contacted the Congdon trustees in March, a few months before the homicides, stating that Marjorie Caldwell..." I breathe deeply and roll my napkin into a tight ball. Tears fill my eyes.

Waller waits patiently.

"Stating that...Marjorie Caldwell was trying to hire a hit man to kill my grandmother."

Waller and Yagoda nod in unison.

"So it's true?"

"Yes," Waller says.

"And there was no security provided for my grandmother?"

"Not to my knowledge," Waller says. "Other than trying to monitor Marjorie Caldwell's behavior."

"That's it?" I say.

No response.

"No one did anything even though they knew about this?"

Waller looks me in the eye.

"I loved my grandmother very much," I say. "This is absolutely heart wrenching."

Waller gives me a minute.

I take a deep breath, and then another. "Okay," I say.

"Did you visit your grandmother often?" Waller asks.

"About six to eight times a year when I was growing up. Once I could drive I would visit her on my own at least every other month."

"Did you ever contact her by phone or mail?"

"I called sometimes but it was difficult for my grandmother to speak due to aphasia," I say. "She had a stroke when I was nine. So I wrote letters and sent cards."

"Are you aware of any items that may have been taken from Glensheen by your mother?"

"You mean stolen?" I ask. I have no idea what's coming.

"Yes," Waller says.

"Not to my knowledge," I say. "But there is something that I've never forgotten."

Yagoda looks at Waller. I don't understand what message they are sending to each other but it doesn't faze me anymore. I know that I'm telling the truth. I think they know it, too. "As a young girl I wrote a letter in friendship to one of my cousins whom I had never met," I say. "The monogrammed stationery was a gift from my grandmother. My nine-year-old cousin wrote, 'You lie and steal and cheat. My parents say so.' I started to cry. I had no idea what she was talking about. None of my siblings or I had ever taken anything from Glensheen. I showed the letter to my grandmother. She shook her head and then she hugged me and told me not to worry. I think it was about eight months before her stroke."

"In 1958, your mother took a painting from the library at Glensheen and sold it," Waller says.

"She stole it?" I say, incredulously.

Waller nods.

I take a minute to do the math. "I would have been four years old."

"The Congdon Office bought it back after it was traced to a gallery in New York. No charges were filed."

Several people walk past our booth. Waller keeps close tabs until they leave the restaurant. "Did you attend the Congdon family reunion in 1975?" he asks.

"I was never told about it. I knew that it was being considered as there hadn't been any type of reunion for many years," I say. "My mother likely received the information but she didn't tell my brothers or sisters or me."

"Your mother was there. Several members of the Congdon family called a security firm because she demanded money. Created trouble."

"She was always trying to ruin things," I say. "Embarrassing everyone, throwing tantrums if she didn't get her way."

Waller reaches for something on his side of the booth. It looks like a photo album. He flips through the pages until he finds what he wants. Then he turns the book so that specific pictures are facing me.

I lean forward trying to get a better look. I immediately recognize the sapphire and diamond ring. "My grandmother wore it every day," I say. But I cringe, realizing that it was stolen off her finger. I readily identify many other pieces: a gold Tiffany pin shaped like a basket with gemstones for flowers, a gold watch, a pearl necklace. But I know something isn't right. "Where's the gold charm bracelet?" I ask. "It has thirteen silhouettes, one for each grandchild."

"We heard about that piece," Waller says. "It was never found."

My heart sinks. "I don't see the emerald and diamond ring either. It had a gold band."

Waller raises his eyebrows and shakes his head back and forth. "No, never found anything like that." He turns the album around and flips though more pages. He finds what he wants and shows me photos of turquoise jewelry. Large stones, nothing Grandma would ever wear.

"I've never seen these before," I say.

"I'm not surprised," Waller says. "These are the Caldwell's pieces."

The paper napkin in my lap is now in shreds.

Next is a picture of a tan garment bag. I can't identify it but I remember the newspaper account. The bag was purchased at a shop in the Minneapolis-St. Paul airport. The recovered sales receipt that was found in the Caldwell's hotel room was dated the day of the homicides.

Waller closes the album. But something is bothering me. The album has triggered something but I don't know what.

"I read that a window was broken at Glensheen," I say. "It was reported to be the point of entry."

"There was a broken window on the lower level," Waller says. "Probably to mislead the investigation."

"Oh my gosh... I just remembered."

Waller waits for me to continue.

Yagoda doesn't move a muscle.

"Did you know that there are photos of every room in Glensheen?" I ask.

"What do you mean?" Waller says, definitely interested.

"An album of photos," I say. "About ten years ago my mother hired a professional photographer. His name is Powell Krueger. She had the staff take my grandmother out for the day so that photos could be taken as a surprise gift. My sister and I are in some of the pictures."

"Pictures of every room in the house?" Waller asks, incredulously.

"Yes, Vera Dunbar told us to go around the estate with the photographer and show him the carriage house, greenhouse, boathouse, and grounds."

"You stated there were pictures of all the rooms," Waller says.

I nod. "Vera Dunbar had already taken the photographer through Glensheen."

"Was your mother there at the time?" Waller asks.

"No, she wasn't. Must have called Vera Dunbar directly." I think for a minute, suddenly horrified. "Vera likely made the decision to take the photographer around the estate without ever notifying anyone in the Congdon Office." I'm suddenly queasy. "Did Vera know of the alleged attempt on my grandmother's life prior to the homicides?" I ask.

"Yes, she did," Waller says.

I rub my temples trying to relieve a pounding headache. "Another red flag, completely ignored," I say.

"Where is the album?" Waller asks.

"The one for my grandmother was kept at Glensheen but I don't know where it is."

"Was there more than one?" Waller asks.

"I know that my mother had a copy made for herself. Vera Dunbar later told me that one of my relatives requested a copy from the photographer as she liked the photos."

Waller eyes Yagoda. "We need to check this out," he says.

Yagoda nods.

"Would you consider testifying if we need you?" Waller asks.

"Yes," I say. "But I have a few more questions."

"Go ahead," Waller says.

"I heard on the news that a will was found in Roger Caldwell's safety deposit box."

"That's right," Waller says. "The will was written and notarized by Marjorie Caldwell three days before the homicides. She had signed over power of attorney to Roger Caldwell, too."

"Murder for hire," I whisper to myself. My heart is racing so fast that I'm lightheaded and dizzy. "What about the private detective?" I ask. "I believe he was hired by one of my relatives who lives in Colorado. By the newspaper accounts he's causing nothing but trouble."

"Furman," Waller says. "One of your relatives hired the private detective, William Furman, on the day of the homicides to protect his family and follow Marjorie and Roger Caldwell."

"How did my relative find this detective?" I ask.

"Said that he got the name from someone within the Colorado Police Department."

"Someone?" I ask.

"He didn't reveal the name," Waller says.

"Have you spoken with Furman?"

"Yes," Waller says.

"What is your opinion of him?"

"Don't trust him," Waller says firmly.

"Was he at Glensheen on the day of the funeral?" I try to recall the faces I didn't recognize.

"No, he wasn't," Waller says.

"So he never intended to do the job," I say.

"Doesn't look like it."

"Are you watching Furman?"

"Yes, we are," Waller says.

The whole thing is a cesspool. Dirtier, murkier, and more suspect than I ever could have imagined.

"Any other questions?" Waller asks.

"No," I say.

"Thank you for your time," Waller says. He hands me a crisp white business card.

Yagoda still hasn't said a word.

I glance at my watch. It's been three hours since we first sat down.

It doesn't take long before I hear the news. On August 5, 1977, five weeks after the homicides, Roger Caldwell is indicted in Duluth by a St. Louis County grand jury on two counts of murder in the first degree. John DeSanto, the prosecuting attorney, assured me that no one would know that I testified briefly, identifying Grandma's jewelry that had been stolen.

I remember the courtroom doors with the bronze brads and kick plates. Tall arched windows and large rectangular skylights illuminated the room. The only people in the courtroom besides me were the court reporter, DeSanto, and the jurors.

As I drove through downtown Duluth after my testimony, the marquee of the Norshor movie theater caught my eye. *You'll Like My Mother,* a murder mystery with modest reviews starring Patty Duke and Richard Thomas, was showing again. It was filmed at Glensheen in 1972.

CHAPTER X

LEARNING TO LIVE

"The best thing for being sad," replied Merlin…"Is to learn
something…learning is the only thing for you."

—T.H. White, *The Once and Future King*

September, 1977

There's a stir in the auditorium. A rustling of papers like the sound of
autumn leaves. Backpacks take up every other upholstered seat. The
identical twins in the nursing program sit three rows in front of me. The
only difference is the side where they part their shiny blond hair.

The teaching assistant strolls in and takes his seat in the front row.
His maroon T-shirt is emblazoned UNIVERSITY OF MINNESOTA in
gold.

"The Krebs cycle takes place inside the mitochondria or 'power
plant' of the cell," the professor says. "It provides energy required for the
organism to function."

Spiral notebooks flap open like the sound of bird wings. I struggle to write every biochemical detail of the eight steps. Oxaloacetate,
citrate, isocitrate, α-ketoglutarate, succinyl-Co-A, succinate, fumarate,
malate. But I quickly realize that I understand what the cycle is and what
it does. The steps make sense.

The words of the upper school principal, Miss Lois Nottbohm, echo in my mind. "You aren't a good enough student," she said when I told her that I wanted to be a nurse. The words *not good enough* echoed over and over. My face flushed as I looked down at my lap. I was determined not to let her see me cry. I had B's in math, Latin, and biology but everything else was a C, D, or sometimes even an E. I wondered just how far down the alphabet the teachers would go.

But Mr. Wayne Haag, at Lakewood Community College, believed in me and I earned an A in Chemistry I and then in Chemistry II.

"For next week please draw the eight steps of the Krebs cycle on a brown paper grocery bag opened flat," the professor says. He flips off the overhead projector and leaves through the door with the red EXIT sign overhead.

I take off jogging across campus as the autumn leaves swirl around me. The smoky smell of fraternity barbecues wafts by. I run past the University of Minnesota buildings named after famous people. I recall the name of the Minnesota State Architect, Clarence H. Johnston, who designed Northrup auditorium and he also designed Glensheen.

The sidewalks are filled with students scurrying to their next class. I dodge through the crowd and dash around the corner to the University of Minnesota Hospital.

The corridors are brightly lit and teeming with activity. Staff physicians and residents in long white coats, nurses with white caps, phlebotomists carrying lab trays with tourniquets trailing from the side, med techs carrying platelet packs from the blood bank, patients pushing IV poles as they walk along the hallway, and social workers with clipboards filled with notes. The air smells medicinal, like Betadine and rubbing alcohol.

As I race to my clinical rotation I wonder if the blindingly handsome James Brolin, who played Dr. Steven Kiley on *Marcus Welby, M.D.,* or the heartthrob Chad Everett, who played Dr. Joe Gannon on *Medical Center*, will magically appear in one of these corridors.

Station 35, the pediatric ward, is filled to capacity. It's a beehive of nurses, doctors, respiratory therapists, and social workers.

I quickly change into a white polyester uniform top and pants and store my street clothes and backpack in a small orange locker before I join six other nursing students. We tightly surround a hospital crib, made of metal bars that look like a miniature prison.

"This child is in a coma secondary to accidental poisoning," the head nurse says. "A gastrostomy tube provides access to the stomach for patients who cannot take nutrition by mouth, are unable to swallow, or need additional supplementation." The G-tube is secured to the child's abdomen with a piece of white gauze and paper tape. I have seen these tubes before, but today I feel queasy and dizzy. Flashing lights and floaters appear in front of my eyes. I blink but the visual pattern is now like exploding fireworks.

The nursing instructor is standing next to the head nurse, who opens a large flow sheet and points to a multitude of tiny squares that contain vital signs, weight, and intake and output. I can hear her explanation but the flashing lights in front of my eyes are so bright that I can't make out her face. All of a sudden everything is dark gray with sparkles like stars.

My legs buckle. Then I fall backwards in slow motion, not even feeling the impact when I hit the floor. The beeping of heart rate monitors, IV pumps delivering medication, and children crying all remind me of where I am.

I open my eyes but the lights are blinding.

Men and women in white coats scurry around me like mice.

"Are you okay, Suzanne?" I hear someone say as if they are in a tunnel.

"Can you hear me?" someone else says.

The room is spinning like I'm on the Tilt-a-Whirl ride at the Minnesota State Fair. A woman with a starched white coat and short red hair puts her face close to mine. She appears to be ten feet tall.

I shiver as she listens to my heart and lungs. Her stethoscope is ice cold. Her breath smells like scrambled eggs.

"She's fine," the woman says abruptly.

The crowd of medical students and residents clears but the nursing students, nursing instructor, and head nurse surround me like I'm road kill.

"These things happen," the nursing instructor says. I wonder if she thinks I can't cut it.

I stand and steady myself against the wall. A blond nursing student straightens the back of my top. I barely know her but I'm grateful. Diane, another student, hands me a glass of orange juice.

I'm barely sleeping. Every night since the homicides I still have the same dream. I hardly eat anything at all. I know that I'll be asked to testify at Roger Caldwell's trial and it won't be under the blanket of secrecy. I wonder just how many people will need to look at the crime scene photos during the investigation and criminal proceedings. Grandma and Velma Pietila passing from hand to hand.

Just the thought of it horrifies me.

It's evening. The phone rings in my one-bedroom apartment in the Kenwood neighborhood of Minneapolis. After the fourth ring I pick up.

"Hello," I say.

"How are you doing?" Pam asks. It's my best friend.

"Fine... other than fainting in my clinical this morning."

"Are you okay?" she asks, genuinely concerned.

"Yes, just embarrassed." I don't want to talk about it and Pam can read me. Her English accent and bubbly laughter have kept me afloat many times. Pam and her husband rode horses and trained with Hans Senn, too. We'd known of each other for several years but it was after the homicides that Pam and I became best friends.

"Just talking to you always makes me feel better," I say. I can just picture her petite frame, short brown hair, and wire rim glasses.

The English sheepdog etching that she made for me still hangs on my wall, nicely framed. Pam started illustrating professionally in 1977. She told me stories about how as a child she drew constantly, incessantly, and on everything that would accept pencil, paint, or charcoal. If she ran out of paper she used the inside of boxes. She drew on cloth, tried birch bark unsuccessfully after reading about Indian tribes, and had stunning results on the television screen.

"Remember the tree you made in your bedroom when you were a little kid?" I ask, trying to think of something other than my bad day.

"You must be talking about the fabulous branches and leaves!" she says.

I laugh as she details how she cut individual leaves, painted each one, and wired them to the branches that climbed across the ceiling of her bedroom. Her mother let her build the round paper tree trunk in the corner.

Pam's childhood was idyllic. She loved to read outdoors so she wouldn't miss anything. She rode Nippy Kicks, the neighbor's dappled gray pony, and she wanted to be an artist, a cowgirl, or a veterinarian. Her favorite name was Dawn.

Pam loved her Grandpa Orville. He was very kind and taught her about the birds, plants, and animals. He gave her a Holstein calf and she named it Domino. Pam and Grandpa Orville rode on the tractor together and they took walks with Perky, the Cocker Spaniel. Grandpa Orville played all sorts of musical instruments. Everyone sang. It didn't matter if they couldn't carry a tune. The most important thing was that everyone in the family was together.

"Thanks for being there," I say.

"Anytime," Pam says.

November, 1977

The Congdon plot has a thick snowy blanket that covers the family. It's so cold my breath forms tiny clouds as I step out of the car. The air is crisp. The wind howls.

Inside the trunk of my car there is a neatly folded child's nursing cape made of bright blue felt with red trim and a brass button at the neck. It was a Christmas gift from Grandma when I was six years old. I wore it during the day and I slept beneath it at night.

I run my fingertips over the soft felt as I hold the cape against my chest along with six pale pink roses.

The black letters of Grandma's headstone peek through the snow. ELISABETH MANNERING CONGDON. She was named after her maternal grandmother, Elizabeth Mannering Bannister. The only difference was in the Old English and German spelling of Elisabeth with an S, which means consecrated of God and set apart for a higher purpose.

Growing up, Grandma's nickname was Sis. Only her two older sisters, Marjorie and Helen, called her by her nickname as an adult. I remember how they would laugh and talk when we ate strawberry shortcake on the Fourth of July.

I gently brush away the snow cover and place the roses in the middle of the granite headstone.

The petals shiver in the breeze.

My hands tremble as I place the little blue cape over the grave fully opened.

The unpredictable winter weather and the steep streets of Duluth will make it difficult to come back until spring. A painful realization, as I've made the two-hour drive every weekend since the funeral.

I lovingly smooth the soft felt with my fingertips. The brass button glimmers in the sunlight.

"I love you, Grandma," I say. "I miss you." The wind tousles my hair.

I close my eyes and think of how nurses are called to protect the living, the dead, and those making the transition. We are the voice for those who cannot speak.

"I will do my best, Grandma," I whisper. "I will be your voice."

Just down the hill a large rectangular monument is sheltered by trees. The granite is covered with leafy gray-blue lichen but the name WOLVIN is still visible. Three headstones are several feet away. Augustus B. Wolvin, Carrie L. Kilgore, wife of Augustus Wolvin, and Fred E. Wolvin.

Captain Augustus Wolvin owned many businesses in the shipping industry, including shipping lines and shipbuilding companies. The Wolvin building in Duluth is named after him.

Fred Eugene Wolvin, the only child of Augustus and Carrie, was four years older than Grandma. He was tall and had brown hair and blue eyes. He worked his way up the ranks and became the manager of the Carnegie Dock and Fuel Company in Duluth, a position he held for many years.

"Fred was a very good dancer," Grandma had told me.

"Was Fred your date?" I asked.

"Yes, a number of times."

"Was his name on the dance card?"

"Yes, his name was there," she said.

Grandma turned down Fred's proposal of marriage, although they remained friends until his death on April 18, 1941, secondary to a coronary thrombus. Fred Wolvin was fifty years old. He had never married and in his will he requested that Grandma wear a ring in honor of their friendship. It was the sapphire and diamond ring that she wore every day.

I bend down and place a large single white rose on the neatly chiseled granite headstone.

"Thank you for loving her," I whisper.

June, 1978

Judge Litman orders a change of venue for Roger Caldwell's murder trial from Duluth, Minnesota, in St. Louis County to Brainerd, Minnesota, in Crow Wing County.

Hordes of media surround the 1920 Beaux Arts courthouse in Brainerd. The first floor exterior is rough-cut stone while the floors above it are smooth-cut gray stone. The front of the building has an arch, cast-iron lampposts, and double glass doors. Dark wood paneling covers the interior walls. The balconied rotunda and marble floors shine as if they are covered with glass.

Opening statements in the trial began almost two months before. Since then, John DeSanto, the Assistant District Attorney, has presented a massive amount of evidence. He's successfully prosecuted at least four homicide cases during his five years on the job; however, the defense has lost no time trying to discredit the police investigation, noting the lack of inventory for the crime scene photos and fingerprints, and noting the failure to protect the crime scene from possible contamination.

"I'll be covering similar material to your testimony at the grand jury hearing," DeSanto says. There's no other preparation.

Detective Gary Waller walks by. He acknowledges my presence with an upward glance.

A court employee whisks me into the brightly lit courtroom. The wood furniture is varnished to a high sheen. I'm quickly sworn in before I take a seat in the witness stand.

I shudder at the sight of Roger Caldwell in a dark suit and tie. He sits quietly at the defense table with Doug Thomson, the renowned criminal attorney.

Caldwell looks toward me.

I look away.

The gallery is filled with spectators but I focus only on DeSanto as he approaches the witness stand. He starts with a few simple questions and then he gets right to the point.

"Miss LeRoy, did you ever know of Roger Caldwell before the homicides?"

"No, sir," I say.

"Are you able to identify Roger Caldwell?" DeSanto asks.

"Yes, sir," I say, as I point to Caldwell. "He's sitting at the defense table."

Roger Caldwell does not react.

"When did you first see Roger Caldwell?"

"The day of my grandmother's funeral."

I hold my shoulders back and concentrate.

"Please describe Roger Caldwell's appearance on the day of the funeral," DeSanto says. He looks me in the eye.

"There was a cut on his upper lip with crusted dried blood," I say. I point to my lip and trace it with my finger. "He held out his right hand. It was very bruised."

"Did Roger Caldwell say anything to you?"

My throat tightens as I recall how frightened I was. But I manage to get the words out. "He said that he was with my mother."

DeSanto nods.

"What is your relationship to Marjorie Caldwell?"

I don't want to say it, but I do. "She's my mother."

"When did you last see Marjorie Caldwell?" DeSanto asks. He runs his fingers over his dark moustache.

"About two years ago," I say. "Other than seeing her at my grandmother's funeral."

DeSanto turns and picks up a large black album. Then he approaches the witness stand and flips to a pre-marked set of photos. He starts with something I know very well.

"Miss LeRoy, could you please identify this ring?"

"It's my grandmother's sapphire and diamond ring."

We go through each piece of jewelry, one by one. The same ones I identified at the grand jury hearing.

"No further questions, Your Honor," DeSanto says.

Doug Thomson approaches the witness stand. The defense attorney has neatly styled gray-flecked hair, wire rim glasses, and a clean-shaven face. His brown three-piece suit with silk tie, gold pocket watch, and gold belt buckle present a polished and expensive looking exterior.

"Miss LeRoy," Thomson says. He doesn't say another word for at least fifteen seconds; simply stares at me.

I turn and glance at the jury. They show no emotion.

"Miss LeRoy," Thomson says again. "You stated that you saw a cut on Roger Caldwell's lip when he approached you."

I nod.

"The witness must verbally respond!" Thomson barks.

My hands are clenched so tightly that my fingernails dig into the flesh of my palms.

The judge looks at me.

I nod my head to let him know that I understand. Then I look at Thomson.

"Yes, sir," I say. "That's correct."

Thomson paces back and forth in front of the witness stand.

I wonder what he's doing and then I realize he's trying to startle me, upset me, and confuse me.

"Miss LeRoy, how close were you to Roger Caldwell when you saw his face?"

"About a foot away," I say.

"You testified that you saw a cut on his upper lip."

"Yes, sir."

"Are you certain that it was a cut?"

"Yes, sir."

"How certain?"

"Very certain," I say. "Dried blood in the shape of a semicircle."

"You testified that you ran away," Thomson says. "How could you see Roger Caldwell's lip?"

"He walked right up to me," I say. "I know what I saw."

Thomson glares at me.

I do not look away. I sit tall in the witness chair.

"Miss LeRoy, did you see your grandmother wear every piece of jewelry that you identified?"

"Yes, sir," I say. "Although she didn't wear all the pieces at the same time or even on the same day."

Thomson returns to the defense table and confers with his foot soldiers.

"No further questions, Your Honor."

I'm surprised. Fewer questions than I thought. However, I'm certain that Thomson knows I'm telling the truth. That I won't budge, not one inch.

I walk out of the courthouse with my head held high.

A photographer races toward me.

I wave him off as I shake my head.

He laughs and simply turns away.

July 8, 1978

Roger Caldwell never testifies on his own behalf. After almost two months of testimony and a little over two days of deliberation, the jury reconvenes. Roger Caldwell is found guilty on two counts of murder in the first degree. Two days later, he is sentenced to two consecutive life terms at Stillwater State Prison in Minnesota.

I breathe a sigh of relief; however, I know that things are about to become very complicated.

CHAPTER XI

FACING THE TRUTH

A good many family trees are shady.
—Robert Elliott Gonzales

July, 1978

It's been two weeks since Marjorie Caldwell was arrested on two counts of aiding and abetting murder in the first degree and two counts of conspiracy to commit murder. I can't even think of her as a mother, much less my own.

I watch to see if anyone at school looks at me differently or seems to recognize me from the testimony at Roger Caldwell's trial. No one says a word if they do. I'm grateful to be camouflaged in the midst of hundreds of students on the University of Minnesota campus.

In the distance, beyond the throngs of students laughing and chatting outside Coffman Union, I catch sight of my friend John. Unmistakable medium build, six feet tall, straight brown shoulder-length hair. A weathered green backpack slung over one shoulder in studied nonchalance. He's just beyond the footbridge that crosses over Washington Avenue.

As he comes closer, I notice his fashionable faded blue jeans and the patina of a wide brown leather belt with a small brass buckle. A neatly ironed blue-and-white-striped Oxford shirt has cuffs folded to mid-forearm.

He waves and I wave back. "Hey," he says. "How are you?"

"I'm good," I say.

Beautiful foliage lines the Mississippi river, flowing beneath the bridge that connects the east and west banks of the massive campus. There's a hint of floral perfume as a group of cheerleaders wearing maroon and gold skirts and matching sweaters run past.

"How's Matt?" I ask. John's longtime partner often joins us for coffee, but not today.

"Just applied to law school," John says.

"That's wonderful."

We make our way to the corner table at a small coffee shop, one room with four tables and chairs. We have the place to ourselves.

"There's something I want to talk to you about," John says. I can tell it's serious by his tone. "Are you doing okay with everything?"

"What do you mean?" I ask. I've only known Matt and John for a few months. Never discussed the legal issues.

"Your grandmother and her nurse," John says quietly. "I've been reading about it in the paper."

I stare out the picture window. Students are racing to class, books in hand. Weathered jean jackets are everywhere. I wonder how long before everyone knows who I am.

"I didn't put it together until I saw your middle name on the class list," John says.

My middle name, Congdon, gave me away. As a little girl, I was so proud of having the same name as Grandma.

John's hand brushes against mine. "I can't even comprehend how you are dealing with this," he says. "Must be brutal."

My chin quivers. "The worst thing is finding something in the paper that I don't already know about. Wondering if people know who I am."

"Hmmmm...like this?" John says.

"Well, yes. Now that you mention it," I say. "But I know that you care."

"Matt and I just want you to be okay," John says. "Do you have support...I mean are there people around when you need them?"

"Yes, when I need them," I say. "But nursing school gives me a lot to think about."

"Is there anyone special?" John asks.

"My grandmother was special," I say.

"I'm sure she was," he says.

The cashier puts a few plastic roses in a glass vase and sets them on the counter.

"I need a lot of time alone," I say. "When I started nursing school I dated a medical student but my life was so busy and so was his." I sigh as I run my finger along the edge of the table. "I'm afraid that a boyfriend could get hurt."

"What do you mean?" John asks. He studies my face.

"You have no idea how malicious the people involved in the criminal case can be." I bristle just thinking about it. "They will stop at nothing to embarrass, intimidate, harass...possibly even cause me harm."

"Why would they do that?"

"Because of the amount of money at stake."

"Sounds like you know firsthand."

I nod. "They would do the same thing to anyone close to me."

"Wasn't there someone else a while back?" John asks. "I think I remember you telling me about him."

"A couple of years ago," I say. "He was a few years older than me and very athletic. We liked to hike and be outdoors. What I loved was that he made me laugh."

"How long were you together?"

"We dated a couple of years but somehow I knew it wouldn't last. My family situation was terrible and I felt responsible for my brother and sisters."

"That's right, the younger kids. I remember now."

"I wanted to go to college and become a nurse and I desperately wanted to travel," I say, as my voice trails off. "We parted as friends."

John nods. "Was there anyone else?"

I shrug. "I dated on and off, but I had so many responsibilities. Now, other than school, my life is mostly dealing with the criminal trials."

I blink back the tears. It was Grandma who showed me how to love and be loved. The men I have dated were kind but they didn't understand my need for independence. I have always known that love is not about control.

"What about hobbies or sports?" John asks, trying to change the subject.

"I cross-country ski and snowshoe in the winter. Hike and canoe in the summer. Even took skeet and trap shooting lessons."

"I had no idea," John says.

"And I really love to travel," I say.

"Where have you been?"

"All over the United States, several countries in Europe, and a polar bear expedition in Canada," I say. "Take off whenever I can. Someday I'm going to Africa, the Orient, and India."

"I'm sure you will."

"I also have a more reflective side."

"Do tell," John says, with a wry smile.

"Tai chi, ikebana, and yoga," I say. "Kind of like meditation."

"My mom does ikebana," John says. "I love the simplicity of Japanese floral design."

Every table now has a glass vase filled with red plastic roses and stems with imitation thorns. John runs his fingertips over the waxy petals.

"Not quite the same," I say.

"Not even close," John says. He turns the vase to see if another angle will improve the presentation. But somehow I know it's not the flowers he's worried about.

"It's great to have outside interests and to be moving forward with your career," he says after a few seconds. "But you need to move forward with your personal life, too."

"I can't risk hurting someone with a situation they can't handle."

"None of this is your fault."

"Guilt by association," I say. "Some of my relatives..."

"What about them?"

"Some of my relatives are very cruel."

"You did nothing wrong."

"So much going on right now," I say. "I'm not trying to find someone. I'm trying to be someone. And someday, I hope that I can do something important with my life."

"You are," John says. "But when you're ready, give yourself and someone else a chance. Take that opportunity."

The thought of a normal life seems years away.

"Promise me," John says.

"I promise that I'll think about."

"Good enough," John says.

May, 1979

The Minnesota Supreme Court orders a change of venue for Marjorie Caldwell's trial from Duluth in St. Louis County to Hastings in Dakota County.

Hastings has an air of things badly out of place. It's been about one month since testimony began. The trial has been a spectacle from the start. DeSanto, the Assistant District Attorney, has tried his best but he's falling deeper into the abyss as the defense discredits each and every shred of evidence.

As I approach the hotel registration area, my radar is fine-tuned. One of Marjorie Caldwell's attorneys is sitting by the front desk looking straight at me. I remember the short dark hair, receding hairline, and muscular build. He clearly knows who I am but he doesn't say a word.

"Checking in?" the desk clerk asks.

"Yes, Suzanne LeRoy," I say, as quietly as I can.

He hands me a room key. "Room 242," he says out loud.

I shudder, wondering if the attorney heard the room number.

As soon as I open the door to my hotel room, the phone rings.

I pick up. "Hello," I say.

"What are you going to testify about?" It's a male voice. I'm certain it's the attorney who was in the lobby.

"Who is this?" I ask.

"What are you going to testify about?" the man barks.

I hang up the phone. It immediately rings. Tentatively, I pick up the receiver.

"What are you going to testify about?"

I hang up the phone.

After five rings I grab the plastic handle of my suitcase, race out of the hotel room, and scramble down the metal stairway that leads to the gravel parking lot in the back of the hotel.

I unlock my car door, jump in, and speed down the road in my blue Pinto. My hands are so clammy that I almost lose my grip on the steering wheel. I check the rear view mirror to see if I am being tailed. There's no one in sight. I notice several hotels along the tree-lined streets but I keep driving until I'm about ten miles away.

Once inside, I check and recheck the dead bolt in the new hotel room. The phone doesn't ring but I don't dare leave out of fear that someone might recognize me.

The next morning my courage fades as I head to the prosecutor's office. One of the defense attorneys is standing at attention in the hallway. He's not the same one that I had seen yesterday, but I've seen this attorney before. Very tall, dark hair, large build, reminds me of Perry Mason.

I shuffle past him without saying a word.

The air is thick but I can still perceive the smoke and mirrors around me.

"One of the attorneys wants to speak to you," John DeSanto says. "Please be polite." Detective Waller is standing beside him.

I can hardly believe it. I realize the defense can ask but I don't have to say anything to them outside the courtroom. I know that.

The defense attorney turns and expects me to follow.

I sweep my shoulder length brown hair off my face and take two steps just outside the doorway, and then I stop. DeSanto and Waller are in earshot. The defense attorney quickly realizes that I'm not going anywhere.

"What are you going to testify about?" he says abruptly. It's definitely not the same voice that I heard over the phone.

I try to look the man in the eye even though he towers above me.

He stares back. It's a showdown.

"I don't have anything to say."

For some reason, the attorney startles.

I feel powerful as I turn and walk back to the prosecutor's office. There's an empty seat and I take my place.

DeSanto and Waller simply stare at me, somewhat astounded.

"I'm not talking to him," I say firmly. I'm determined to protect myself if no one stands up for me. I wait for words of preparation for today's testimony. There aren't any.

DeSanto gets up from his chair in the courthouse office and picks up a large black satchel just as a man in a brown two-piece suit enters the room.

"Mark, please take Suzanne to the waiting area," DeSanto says to his associate.

The man nods. He looks at me and tries to smile. It's clearly an effort. Everyone is on edge.

I'm escorted down a long hallway and then I'm left alone in the formal courthouse library, surrounded by hundreds of law books. I know this is going to be rough. In 1881, Great-grandfather Chester was appointed Assistant United States Attorney in Minnesota, a position he held until 1886. I wish that he were here. I know that he would help me. He would know what to do.

I close my eyes for a few seconds. Just as I open them, I hear a voice.

"Suzanne, we're ready for you."

The courtroom is right off the law library. The bright lights blind me as I step through the doorway. It feels as if I'm on stage.

Marjorie Caldwell is seated at the defense table right in front of me. Just the sight of her short dark hair and large round glasses is terrifying.

There's a soft murmur in the courtroom as I walk to the witness stand. I glance at the jury. They look away. They're not sympathetic. I hold up my right hand and I am sworn in. The witness stand has an oak chair with a swivel. I sit as quietly as I can but my legs are trembling. The chair rotates. I try to stay still but the chair keeps moving.

DeSanto approaches me. Just as quickly, he turns and walks away. I have no idea what he's doing. Then he steps back to his table and picks up the yellow legal pad that he's forgotten. He straightens his suit coat and tries to pump up a little dignity. The defense has created doubt about everything. Endless newspaper accounts point to Furman, the rogue private investigator who was hired by a member of the Congdon family; lost evidence, lack of inventory documentation by the police, and fingerprint evidence on an envelope that was allegedly used by Roger Caldwell to mail the stolen Byzantine coin to his home address. Experts for the defense have testified that the fingerprint on the envelope is not a match to Caldwell's fingerprint even though it was presented into evidence by the State. The newspapers predict bad things for the prosecution.

I wait for DeSanto. There's nothing else I can do.

He walks toward me, legal pad in hand. After several general questions he gets to the point. "Miss LeRoy, what is your relationship with Marjorie Caldwell?"

"Marjorie Caldwell is..." I feel like I will choke. "My mother."

"Please elaborate," DeSanto says.

My heart is racing. "We barely spoke," I say. I remember the same feeling as a little girl. Not wanting to tell the story about what happened in our house. But now I must tell the story for Grandma and Velma Pietila.

I run my hand down the front of my red dress, trying to feel its power.

"My mother lied to me all the time," I say. "I never knew what she was going to do to me or to my younger siblings."

The courtroom is eerily silent.

"Miss LeRoy, please describe Marjorie Caldwell's spending habits," DeSanto says.

"New horses were shipped to the barn without any notice," I say. "Boxes of custom-made riding coats were constantly being shipped to the house."

DeSanto quickly moves on. "Miss LeRoy, are you aware of any fires that occurred in your home when you were growing up?"

"Yes, sir," I say. "There were two in the house. Back-to-back on the same day." I remember the smell of charred wood. The firemen in yellow coats tinged with gray ash and the terrified faces of the neighbors. I can almost feel my eyes burn from the smoke. "About a year later there was a fire in the garage."

There's a stir among the spectators in the gallery.

"And there was a fire after that," I say. "At a newly built home on Marine on St. Croix."

DeSanto nods. He does not ask me to elaborate. He moves quickly to the photo album. Once again I am asked to identify Grandma's jewelry, piece by piece.

"No further questions, Your Honor," DeSanto says.

The defense is next. Ron Meshbesher, a top criminal attorney in the Midwest, approaches the witness stand. His full beard and moustache complement his curly brown hair flecked with gray. I scan his three-piece designer suit and large dark-rimmed glasses.

He blinks at me with disdain.

A brigade of assistants pushes files around the defense table. A young female defense attorney sneers at me. Marjorie Caldwell laughs and whispers to her team. It's a nest of serpents.

"Miss LeRoy, isn't it true that you refused to visit your grandmother when your mother asked because you were riding in horse shows?"

I look straight at Meshbesher, wanting to see him sweat. "No sir, that's not true. I visited my grandmother often and on my own," I say, trying to remain calm. "When I rode in horse shows my mother was always there."

Meshbesher frowns. He turns and scans the jury. They follow his every move. There seems to be an unspoken exchange.

"You testified that your mother lied to you," Meshbesher says.

"Yes, sir."

"So she lied all the time. Never told the truth."

"She lied so much that I never knew when she was telling the truth."

Meshbesher paces in front of the witness stand. There's a hint of after-shave.

"Miss LeRoy, why is it that you never gave your grandmother gifts?"

"Sir, I did give my grandmother gifts. Many different times." Needlepoint pillows, books, embroidery, and a hand-knit sweater all flash before me.

"Why is it that there's no record of it in the gift book?"

"I don't know of any gift book," I say.

Meshbesher stares me down.

I hold my ground. He does not offer a gift book as evidence because there isn't one. It's a repertoire of dirty tricks.

"Isn't it true that your mother made a large needlepoint rug as a gift for your grandmother?" Meshbesher asks. "It had all the state birds and a large eagle in the center."

"Yes, sir. That's correct," I say. "But I heard from Vera Dunbar that Marjorie Caldwell took it the day of the funeral and sold it."

"Do you know that for a fact, Miss LeRoy?"

"I believe Vera Dunbar," I say.

Meshbesher slaps his hand against the defense table. The sound of flesh echoes throughout the courtroom.

I startle but I am determined to stay strong.

Meshbesher unbuttons his suit coat. A large silver belt buckle shines in the brightly lit courtroom. The defense attorney turns toward the jurors and places his hands in his pockets. There seems to be another unspoken exchange.

The seasoned warhorse turns and faces me. "Miss LeRoy, can you tell the court the date of your grandmother's birthday?" he asks. "Do you even know?"

Stunned by the arrogance, I feel dizzy. The courtroom is a blur. I'm desperate to be accurate but a nagging sense of self-doubt overcomes me. I concentrate. I'm certain it's April 22, 1894. Great-grandmother Clara's birthday is April 29, 1854. The days are one week apart.

"April 22, 1894," I say. I know I'm right.

"No further questions, Your Honor," Meshbesher says.

DeSanto sits in his chair. Shoulders slumped forward. His face is pale. I believe he's doing his best. I have to believe it.

I tried to be the voice for Grandma and Velma Pietila but I sink a bit in the witness chair because I don't think it was good enough.

But the next day I receive a letter with a Duluth, Minnesota, postmark. I admire the light-blue envelope and lovely penmanship, hoping that it's a friendly note. It is. The daughter of Grandma's second oldest brother, Ned, sends her love and support. I read her words over and over. "Your grandmother would have been very proud."

Dr. Elizabeth Colville Bagley is barely five feet tall. Grandma's friend and former physician is a tiny woman with a magnanimous presence. Large glasses frame dark serious eyes. She is one of three physicians in the Bagley family, the first female surgeon in Duluth, and a former chief of staff at St. Luke's Hospital. When I was a little girl, she let me look in her black doctor's bag. I saw the stethoscope, cotton, bandages, tongue depressors, and a little light to look in her patient's eyes and ears.

It's only a few days after my testimony and it's the first time that I have seen Dr. Bagley since Grandma's funeral.

"Suzanne, I'm so glad that you wanted to come," Dr. Bagley says.

"Thank you so much for inviting me," I say.

We sit on a firm sofa in the living room of her beautiful brick house on East Third Street, about twelve blocks from Glensheen. Sunlight streams through the windows. Flowers and green plants adorn the room. I try to gather my thoughts about what is bothering me. What I need to know.

Dr. Bagley pours us each a cup of tea. The Wedgwood teapot has a beautiful floral design.

"My mother has been unruly and frightening ever since I can remember," I say. I can barely get the words out fast enough. "Ever since the homicides I have wondered what I could have done to protect my grandmother."

"There was absolutely nothing you could have done," Dr. Bagley says, emphatically.

"I have to think it was something genetic, something that went terribly wrong," I say. "A tangle of DNA and evil that is beyond comprehension."

"Marjorie was adopted as an infant and even so, we often never know all the factors," Dr. Bagley says. "Your grandmother provided a warm, loving, and financially stable home to both of her daughters."

"I heard that her brothers were involved as the girls grew up."

"Yes, Ned and Robert and her brother-in-law, Harry Dudley. They were wonderfully supportive as were her mother and sisters. None of the parenting risk factors were there although your grandmother felt that maybe she was inconsistent with discipline."

"My grandmother was very loving to my siblings and me," I say. "She role-modeled manners, decorum, and values. My brothers and sisters and I learned by watching her example. We wanted her to be proud of us."

"She was very proud of all of you," Dr. Bagley says.

I struggle to hold back the tears.

"Your grandmother often tried to think of what she might have done differently," Dr. Bagley says. "Marjorie had behavioral problems as a child and as she got older they became worse. She always seemed to have difficulty with money."

"Was she ever evaluated?" I ask. "I've heard rumors but nobody talks about it."

"After Marjorie completed her junior year of high school your grandmother took her to the Menninger Foundation. A world-renowned psychiatric facility and clinic in Topeka, Kansas."

I think for a minute. "The evaluation would have been in 1949 if she had completed eleventh grade. She would have been seventeen at the time," I say. "What was the diagnosis?"

"I wasn't your mother's physician; however, your grandmother and I discussed the diagnosis. Conduct disorder."

"That's it?"

"Sounds benign, but it isn't," Dr. Bagley says. "It's a long-standing violation of rules and anti-social behavior." She looks me in the eye. "There's something I want to be sure you understand, Suzanne. None of this is your fault. There's nothing you could have done. I think that many members of the Congdon family wonder what they could have done. There were many, many red flags."

I nod. "I looked up sociopath and psychopath but they aren't diagnoses," I say. "It sounds like sociopaths sometimes feel empathy but psychopaths never do."

"That's right. Sociopaths and psychopaths are descriptors of behaviors, not diagnoses of personality disorders. However, it doesn't mean the behaviors Marjorie exhibited weren't a significant concern."

"I understand," I say. "But now it appears that she has every characteristic of a psychopath."

"Yes," Dr. Bagley says. "It does." She pours us both another cup of Earl Gray tea. "If I remember correctly Marjorie attended twelfth grade at a special school in St. Louis. I believe it was associated with Menninger."

"She would have graduated in 1950, I think, just before she turned eighteen," I say.

"I believe that's right," Dr. Bagley says.

"One of my relatives and my father apparently told the media that my mother went to college in St. Louis, but the stories don't match. One said it was Washington University and the other said it was St. Louis University."

"Your grandmother had a difficult time finding out exactly what your mother was doing at that time," Dr. Bagley says.

"I checked with both colleges. My mother never registered or attended either one," I say. "Likely no one knew the truth."

"Marjorie became engaged to your father just a few months after they met," Dr. Bagley says. "Your grandmother wanted your mother to travel and complete her education but Marjorie refused. Six months later, your mother and father were married and everyone hoped things would get better."

"But they didn't," I say.

"No, they didn't."

"My grandmother built a foundation for me and I knew that even if no one else loved or cared about me, she always did."

"Yes, she absolutely did," Dr. Bagley says.

"I wanted to thank you for taking such wonderful care of her for so many years," I say. "I know that..." I hesitate for a minute. "I know that you were with her during the autopsy. I read about it in the paper and it gave me a great deal of comfort."

"It was my duty and privilege," Dr. Bagley says. "I was ten years older than your grandmother but we were long-time friends." Her face lights up. "We used to canoe on the Brule with the Marshall sisters. Everyone called me 'Skipper' because I was so good with a paddle."

I admire the beautiful green plants and flowers that add natural beauty to the lovely room. I think for a minute and then I say the inevitable.

"I'm worried that my mother will get off and that she'll hurt someone else. All I want is for justice to be served."

"That's all we can hope for," Dr. Bagley says.

A red-winged blackbird lands on a bush just outside the window. It's watching and waiting just like everyone else.

July 21, 1979

It's late afternoon. I struggle to loosen the knot in my shoelace, a death grip of my own creation.

Suddenly the phone rings.

I feel uneasy as I race to pick up. Marjorie Caldwell's verdict is in the hands of the jurors.

"The news isn't good," Pam says. "She was acquitted on all charges."

I can barely breathe. I'd hoped things would be different even though I knew that it was unlikely. The defense created reasonable doubt about everything and Marjorie Caldwell never testified.

"I'm sorry this happened," my best friend says.

"Those jurors have absolutely no idea what they've unleashed," I say. The frantic pace of my heart echoes with every word I speak. It's like a message in Morse code telling me not to give up.

"I know, but there's nothing you can do," Pam says.

"Actually, there is..."

"What do you mean?"

"I could start a civil suit."

Silence.

"What does that do?"

"It prevents Marjorie Caldwell from receiving her inheritance if she's found guilty in a civil court," I say. "I believe that it's based on preponderance of evidence instead of 'beyond a reasonable doubt' like a criminal case."

"How do you know all this?" Pam asks.

"I spoke with a law student at the University of Minnesota but never divulged who I am. He showed me where I could look up the information."

I remember flipping through the pages of the thick book, talking to the law librarian and a legal advisor, all incognito. I wanted to be prepared just in case the verdict turned out as it has. I know that I can handle a civil suit even though there are many nights when I barely sleep, and days when I feel like I'm always looking over my shoulder. Sometimes I eat a few Cheerios for breakfast but nothing more and other days when I eat three donuts and a pizza, always trying to outwit the scale because there's nothing else that I can control.

"More attorneys and legal issues," Pam says. "Won't be easy."

I know she's right but there's a gnawing sensation that I know will never go away if I don't move forward. "I can't live with myself if I don't do this," I say. "There's so much those jurors don't know. My grandmother protected me over and over. I have to do what I know is right."

"Chris and I support you," Pam says. "We're here for you."

It's the one thing I know for sure.

PART III

BIRD OF SHADOWS

CHAPTER XII

ABSENCE OF CIVILITY

It is only when we have the courage to face things exactly as they are… that a light will develop out of events, by which the path to success may be recognized.

—*I Ching*

July, 1979

It's barely a week after the verdict.

"A meeting has been scheduled with a Minneapolis attorney," my brother tells me over the phone. "The end of this week."

"What about?" I ask.

"I think it's to discuss the outcome of the trial," he says.

"We know the outcome of the trial," I say. "Who arranged this?"

"Uncle Chuck called me. He'll probably call you, too." It's been years since I have seen or spoken to Mom's sister or her husband. I don't trust this at all.

"Is this about a civil suit?" I ask. I know that my brothers and sisters and I are the only ones who can pursue a case to disinherit our mother.

"Don't know," Pete says.

The next day the phone rings.

"Suzanne, it's Uncle Chuck." The deep voice is vaguely familiar.

Silence.

"Your mother was found not guilty," he says.

"Yes, I'm aware of that," I say.

"A great deal of money is involved," he says. There it is. Bottom line.

"Apparently there's a meeting next week at a Minneapolis attorney's office," I tell him.

"Yes, and you should go," he says.

I wonder how he would have known about the meeting unless he was involved with the arrangements.

August, 1979

The civil attorney smiles condescendingly as he surveys the room. The hardwood chairs in front of his desk are filled with four of my siblings and me. Two of my brothers aren't here. They've aligned with Mom and her defense team.

The attorney leans back, hands clasped behind his neck. "As you know, Marjorie Caldwell was acquitted," he says.

My brothers and sisters don't say a word.

"Who arranged this meeting?" I ask.

No answer.

"Did someone hire you?"

The attorney folds his arms across his chest and simply stares at me.

"Whoever it is, this isn't their case," I say.

"A great deal of money is at stake," the attorney says.

There it is again.

"An option for you kids is to begin a civil suit."

"Please don't call us that," I say.

"What do you mean?" the attorney says.

"Kids," I say. "Please don't call us that."

My siblings stare at me.

"Does anyone want to participate in a civil suit?" the attorney asks.

My siblings shake their heads back and forth.

"If your mother is found guilty in a civil court she would not be entitled to her inheritance. The money would then pass to all of you," the attorney says. He's not about to let this slide by.

My sisters stare straight ahead.

One of my brothers clears his throat.

I bristle.

Ken Maine of the Congdon Office has told me about the trusts in question and the multi-million dollar estate. He's mentioned interest in a generation-skipping trust that was set up by Great-grandfather Chester, and properties in Arizona and Wisconsin. He expressed concern about others who may try to take the money in less than honorable ways under adverse circumstances.

I know that no one can proceed with a civil suit other than my siblings and me, individually or together. We're the only ones who would benefit. The only problem is that I don't have the funds to hire my own attorney. The entire situation feels shady.

"You kids need to do this," the attorney says emphatically.

"We're adults," I say. "You need to treat us respectfully." I have yet to understand how control over the case will be wrestled away. Demeaning us may be the start.

The attorney leans back in his chair. The smirk on his face is unchanged.

I wonder what the plan is, how many people are behind the smoke and mirrors, how many attorneys it will take, and how many handlers there will be.

"I never asked you to represent me," I say abruptly. "I need to consider my options."

The attorney sits upright in his chair. I am his immediate problem.

He looks at my siblings. "Are you sure you don't want to be part of this?" he asks them pointedly.

They all say, "No."

I wrestle with the issues over the next few days. Marjorie Caldwell will never go to jail for the homicides. The jurors in the criminal trial made sure of that. My only recourse is a civil case.

I pick up the phone and call the attorney, knowing that all my faculties will need to be finely tuned. "I would consider proceeding with the case," I say. "However, it would have to be on my terms."

"I'll get the paperwork together," he says, not letting me get a word in edgewise. I can almost see him smiling through the phone.

I suspect that he calls whoever is involved but I can't prove it.

Nobody's talking.

"Please be a part of this," I beg my younger sisters for the tenth time. I know that the civil case will be stronger if at least one of my siblings is involved. But I've already decided to go forward by myself if necessary.

"Fine, put my name on the case," Becky says. "But I'm not doing anything."

"I'll take care of it," I say.

"Okay, but I don't want to be responsible," Heather says. "Not for anything." She sighs heavily, almost a groan.

"You won't," I say.

My brothers don't want any part of the case and not one of them wants to talk about it.

One week after the meeting with the attorney, a crisp white contract arrives in the mail. A contract was never discussed.

I read every word but it's the final sentence that stands out. *Pending successful completion of a civil trial, an unknown percentage of the funds will be taken.* It's a black hole of greed and deceit. Exactly what I was afraid would happen.

The blood drains from my face as I wonder if my sisters received the same contract.

Horrified, I race to the phone and dial Heather's number first.

"Don't sign the contract," I say, when she picks up.

"I'm not doing anything," Heather says. "Just opened it."

"I have to call Becky," I say. "Gotta go."

Becky picks up the phone after the first ring.

"Don't sign any contract," I say. "The civil attorney is trying to pull a fast one."

"Who is this?" she says.

"It's me," I say. "Your sister."

I can hear her tearing open the envelope. "I'm sick of all this," she says. "I don't even understand what he's talking about."

That's exactly the point, I think to myself. "Please, just let me handle it."

"Okay, fine," she says crossly.

I know that I need to move forward with the case but not this way. With bold strokes of a Magic Marker I obliterate the last paragraph of the contract. Beneath the sinister sentences I sign the line at the bottom of the page and mail it back.

The next day the attorney calls. "Suzanne, you need to come into the office," he barks.

"Why is that?" I ask, knowing full well that he is unhappy.

"You need to sign the contract without blacking anything out."

"I'm not doing that."

"We have to talk about this," he says.

"About what? Your firm and others taking everything?" I say. "My great-grandfather worked very hard to earn this money and my grandmother protected it."

I remember the letter Grandma showed me. On June 30, 1880, Great-grandfather Chester wrote to Great-grandmother Clara, his fiancée at the time. It was a difficult time in his life but he sent Clara the first five-dollar bill that he ever earned as an attorney. "I hope that a good many will follow," he wrote. He was worried about his prospects; however, in 1881 his fortune began to change when he was appointed Assistant United States Attorney for Minnesota. Not long after, on September 29, 1881, Chester and Clara were married.

"Come in to discuss it!" the attorney yells.

"I'm not signing it," I say, holding my ground.

"Please, come in to discuss it," the attorney says. His demeanor has suddenly changed.

Against my better judgment I agree to an appointment the next day, wanting to see if his position has softened.

A fresh contract is immediately slapped on the table. The attorney leans forward and hands me a shiny back pen.

I move my chair back and shake my head. "I thought we were going to discuss this," I say. "If not, I'm leaving."

"Clearly, you don't understand how these things work," he says.

"I understand these things *very* clearly," I say. "Much more than you think. Now what's the percentage?"

"I don't know what percentage we would take," the attorney says.

"Why not?"

No answer.

"Who else is involved?" I ask. "It's my uncle, isn't it?"

No response.

"What's the percentage?" I ask again.

"I don't know."

"So, one hundred percent. You'd take it all."

"I didn't say that," the attorney says. "A percentage is normally agreed on."

"Then I'd like to know the percentage that you're thinking."

"No!" he says. His face is beet red.

"Then I'm not signing it," I say. "You have no case without me. I'm well aware of that."

I get up and leave without signing the contract.

The next day I receive a fresh contract in the mail. I stare at the last sentence. *Pending successful completion of the civil case, an unknown percentage will be taken.* I read it over and over again, trying to figure out what to do.

Then I see it. The gaping loophole is right in front of me. The key is in the first part of the final sentence. *Pending successful completion of the civil case,* an unknown percentage will be taken. If the civil case never goes to trial there will never be an issue with anyone taking an unknown percentage. How could this have been overlooked? Did they really think that I wouldn't figure it out?

I'll do my best to prevent Marjorie Caldwell from being rewarded and still prevent the unknown percentage issue from ever seeing daylight.

I realize there's no way around the fact that she will receive some of the funds if a settlement occurs but likely the majority of her share would go to pay millions of dollars or more that she owes her defense attorney. I have no idea what she would do with whatever is left of her share other than spend it immediately. But I have no control over that.

What I can do is make sure the case never goes to trial. That's what I do have control over. If I withdraw from the civil suit at a key time it will force a settlement. I'm certain of that because the financier, whoever it is, will want their money back and the law firm will not want to be held accountable for the fees.

I sign the contract and mail it in. No black marks through the last paragraph.

"Suzanne, I see that you thought this through," the attorney says when he calls.

I certainly did, I think to myself.

"I'm going to arrange a meeting," the attorney says.

"For what reason?" I ask.

"So we can meet with your uncle." I can feel the knife in my back already.

"So my uncle is funding the case?"

No response.

"I'm going to ask you one more time," I say. "I signed the contract, now I want to know."

The attorney sighs. "Your uncle agreed to pay the attorney fees because the case may take a long time. He will be reimbursed if the case is successful."

"Why wouldn't you discuss this with me when I asked?"

"Because we thought it would be better this way."

"We?" I ask

No response.

"Did my uncle approach you about taking this case? About representing him?"

No response.

I know he won't answer but I keep firing off questions.

"What else will be taken from the unknown percentage?" I ask. I start to wonder if they will charge interest.

The silence is deafening.

"So, you've been planning this all along, excluding me from the conversation," I say.

The civil attorney and any others who may be involved besides my uncle clearly think they have the reins. That may be true, but only for a while. I have a plan and no one has a clue.

It's not long before a newspaper article with aerial photos implies that I have more than a professional relationship with Hans Senn, the horse trainer.

I strain to see between the lines. So this is how the other side comes after me, how Marjorie Caldwell and her defense team will try to make me back down from the civil suit so I won't try to disinherit her.

Hans is thirty years older than I am. He's a father figure, devoted friend, and confidant, nothing more.

My friends in the horse world surround me. As grateful as I am, I realize more than ever that anyone associated with me will also be at risk. It's clear the defense will stop at nothing.

The civil attorney comes out to the stable, "To investigate," he says. I have told him there's no truth to the accusations but the car door opens and he steps out. Flannel shirt, jeans, and leather boots. Certainly dresses the part.

"Why don't we go to my office," Hans says.

We sit in a semicircle in a sun-filled room with a large picture window. Horses are grazing in the paddocks nearby.

"There's no truth to any of these accusations," Hans says.

"Suzanne said the same thing," the attorney says. "Could I see where she lives?"

"Why don't you ask her?" Hans says matter-of-factly.

The building where I live is visible in the distance. The old stable was renovated into apartments on the opposite end of the property, half a mile from the house where Hans lives.

"Can I see it?" the attorney says to me.

"See what?" I ask. "My apartment?"

"Yes," the attorney says.

"What for?" I ask.

"I'd just like to see where you live."

His arrogance astounds me.

I glance at Hans. "It's up to you," he says.

"I want Hans to come with us," I say. "The employees who live in the building didn't ask for their privacy to be invaded."

The attorney nods.

The three of us follow the tire tracks on the long gravel driveway as we make our way on foot.

The screen door at the end of the building squeaks.

The carpeted hallway is immaculate. The attorney doesn't even wipe his feet after he steps inside. My apartment is the first door on the right. Fumbling with my keys, I find the correct one.

The attorney steps up right behind me.

Angry, I turn around and stare him down.

He takes one step back.

I insert the key, turn it, and barely open the door before the attorney steps in front of me. He takes one look and laughs. "I had a hole-in-the-wall like this when I was a law student," he says.

Suddenly embarrassed, my cheeks feel singed as if I'm too close to a blazing fire. I scan the room. A small sofa is tucked in the corner and there's a table and chairs, refrigerator, toaster oven, wood cabinets, and neatly made bed with a bright comforter. The floor is carpeted. Closets extend along one side of the room. Paneled walls are decorated with framed pictures.

"Is there a problem?" Hans snaps at the attorney. He could take the guy. I just know it.

The attorney flushes. "No," he says. Apparently it's not so funny anymore.

I have no idea why he wants to embarrass me. But then I realize that it's all about control. The collective shadow of human predators is like thick, toxic air that suffocates me. But I will not back down.

As the attorney heads back to his car, he scuffs his new leather boots and stops to examine the scratches. Not a rugged outdoor enthusiast. The blue jeans are way too stiff and the plaid shirt still has creases from the store.

I wonder how many people will hear his impression of where I live. I don't mention that I will be moving to a one-bedroom apartment near the University of Minnesota campus in two weeks. I don't tell him that the drive is too far to commute due to extensive clinical demands during my final year of nursing school. I don't tell him because he does not treat me respectfully. I don't tell him because he does not deserve to know.

CHAPTER XIII

NURSING THE SICK

You must never think of anything except the need,
and how to meet it.
—Clara Barton

November, 1982

It's been almost three years since I graduated from nursing school and passed the licensure exam. It seems like ages since my first clinical when I fainted in the pediatric unit, and the psychiatric clinical in the locked unit during which the troubled adolescent started beating her head against the table and had to be restrained by two orderlies. I remember the circular scars with ragged edges that were scattered over the back of her hands, a result of cigarette burns inflicted when she was a child, a sleeve of tattoos covering each arm, multiple healed cuts in a distinct pattern on her legs, a total of sixteen piercings in her ears, nose, eyebrows, and lips. I remember the epidemiology paper that I wrote on the wrong topic, Sickle Cell Anemia instead of Sickle Cell Trait, and the kindness of the doctoral student who taught the class. He told me that doctors, nurses, and scientists all learn from their mistakes.

I flourished in my clinical training, working with vulnerable and marginalized populations. Now my patients are the smallest and most critically ill infants in the Neonatal Intensive care Unit (NICU) at the University of Minnesota Hospital. Many are premature and others have a wide variety of congenital anomalies.

The NICU is brightly lit. Monitors sound an alarm with every missed beat of tiny hearts. Respirators hum. I check and re-check minute medication doses, monitor IV fluids, suction endotracheal tubes, draw blood gases, evaluate lab results, manage central lines, and measure dialysate. During cardiac arrests, chest compressions are administered over hearts the size of a walnut. But it's so much more than the technical aspects. It's the nurses who mentored me, shared their skills, and helped me to gain confidence. Their years of experience and generous sharing of kindness, patience, and expertise have taught me about family-centered nursing care as well as collegiality as a form of service to each other. I will always be grateful.

However, in the midst of finding my own place among the nurses, there isn't a day that I don't think about Velma Pietila and the sacrifice she made trying to protect Grandma in the line of duty. Her cremated remains were returned to her loving family on July 29, 1977, after her memorial service. I have struggled with how to pay my respects, how to honor her life. I haven't found the right way because I am so filled with my own grief and I feel guilty for thinking of myself instead of what her family is going through and the loss they must endure.

Earlier this month, in November, 1982, Loren Pietila, Velma's husband, and their children, filed a wrongful death suit for $475,490 due to lack of security at Glensheen. The front gates to the estate had been open. No security system had been installed and there was no security guard or drive-by surveillance. Just a few weeks back, in mid-November, jurors in the case quickly found the Congdon trustees and conservators liable for Velma Pietila's death and they awarded her family $225,000.

Marjorie Caldwell's acquittal in the criminal trial prevents her from being liable. The Congdon trustees have now taken the case to the Minnesota Supreme Court. I can't even comprehend how the value of a life can be calculated in terms of dollars.

I think back to my graduate clinical this morning, when I cared for a sixteen-year-old patient who is alone and seven months pregnant with no prior prenatal care. It's her fourth pregnancy, unplanned like the previous three and complicated by premature contractions, gestational diabetes, and hepatitis B. A green-and-blue tinged bruise with streaks of yellow surrounded her bloodshot left eye. Her hands were clenched against her chest. As she slept, I wondered how many invisible bruises there were. The quiet cries for help.

Every day I see patients struggling with poverty, addiction, low expectations, hopelessness, and trauma but I also see the promise of possibility. My patients are teaching me to stop and listen to the silence within and I realize that I need to tend to my own wounds and not look away.

The pattern of sleepless nights and the dream that recurs when I do manage to sleep continues to dominate my life. It's the same dream every night since the homicides, in which I run down an endless black asphalt driveway but my bare feet don't touch the ground. The details of the long white sleeveless gown flowing like chiffon behind me, and the crimson stain over my heart are etched in my mind.

I gaze at the stacks in the university's Wilson Library, the one that specializes in the arts, humanities, and social sciences. After picking one of many books on symbolism I learn that images are grounded in experience, that they often express what cannot be said, and they unfold with new meanings over time. The psychologist Carl Jung believed that dreams are a window to the unconscious. Dreams, in his view, serve to guide and offer a solution to a problem you are facing in your waking life.

As I lean against the wall in a secluded corner I try to attach significance to my own life experience with the experiences and beliefs of others in the world. The innocence and purity of the white dress represents the color of mourning in many cultures. The red stain is the trauma and heartbreak in my life. Feet are said to represent the soul and bare feet are a manner of respect, such as removing shoes before entering a room or a holy place. Running feet represent the effort to move on instinct, trying to re-establish contact with the ground after distress and misery. Silence is the effort to eradicate or handle tension in life. The endless winding driveway represents instability and many hindrances.

It's quiet. I close my eyes for a minute but I can't concentrate on the dream anymore. In the back of my mind I know that I have to focus on my master's thesis, a study of babies with congenital cardiac anomalies.

I zip up my winter jacket and I brave the howling winds and snow flurries. The Biomedical Library is a few blocks away. Once inside, I glimpse an iridescent light peeking through the stacks and I follow the rainbow of colors to a table covered with medical journals.

As I flip through the pages I think back to the most pressing public health issues in Grandma's era. In Minnesota at the turn of the twentieth century, four out of ten mothers experienced the death of a child. One out of every ten children died before one year of age. For every hundred live births an average of seven women in the United States died of pregnancy-related complications.

Grandma was the 423rd child born in St. Louis County in 1894, in the fashionable East End of Duluth. Brimming with health, she had brown hair and brown eyes and weighed eight and a half pounds. She was one of the lucky ones blessed with good health in an era when there were no antibiotics and no vaccines.

I recall how Grandma used her leadership and training to support the King's Daughters, an ecumenical Protestant group dedicated to silent service, and it was here that her activism in maternal-child health took off. In the mid-twentieth century the King's Daughters provided a day nursery at the F.A. Patrick Company, one of the foremost woolen manufacturers in Duluth and northern Minnesota, with baby clinics and weighing days in an effort to decrease infant mortality from diarrhea, dehydration, and infectious disease. In 1915 there were 538 baby clinics in the United States, five times more than in 1910 when the National Association for the Study and Prevention of Infant Mortality was formed.

I think of the myriad of maternal-child health issues as I flip through more public health journals. I come across a picture of Margaret Sanger, the founder and first president of Planned Parenthood. She was the sixth of eleven children. Her mother, Anne, had multiple miscarriages and ended up dying from tuberculosis at age fifty. Margaret subsequently attended nursing school in the Catskills; she opened the first birth control clinic in a tenement in Brooklyn, New York, in October of 1916. She was promptly arrested, tried, and found guilty for creating a public nuisance, and later served a 30-day sentence in a penitentiary for women in Queens, New York, in 1917. Her efforts to gain government support for birth control failed until 1936 when a ruling by the U.S. Court of Appeals gave doctors the right to prescribe and dispense contraceptives by exempting them from the Comstock Law.

Following Margaret Sanger's lead in 1936, Grandma and her personal physician, Dr. Elizabeth Bagley, helped start a family planning clinic in Duluth, which eventually became a Planned Parenthood clinic.

I begin to realize just how closely my nursing trajectory is intertwined with the path Grandma forged. In a few months I will begin post-graduate training as an OB/GYN nurse practitioner at Planned Parenthood in St. Paul.

Before I leave the library, I pick up today's newspaper from one of the tables. As I scan the pages my skin tingles like a million tiny pinpricks all over my body.

On January 16, 1983, Marjorie Caldwell was arrested for suspected arson at her home in Mound, Minnesota. After making the $20,000 bail she was released. I hadn't even known she was living in Minnesota again.

I shudder as I try to picture whether or not I locked the door to my car before I left the parking ramp this morning.

I keep reading. Investigators incidentally discovered that Marjorie Caldwell committed bigamy in North Dakota two years earlier on August 8, 1981. She was not extradited due to cost of prosecution, although she was advised never again to set foot in North Dakota, where she'd married a man named Wally Hagen while her husband, Roger Caldwell, was serving time in prison. The name Wally Hagen is strangely familiar. It takes me a moment to put it together. My brother Steve and I figure skated with the Hagen children when we were growing up. Their mother, Helen Hagen, was a nurse.

A few students are lingering at the information desk on the other side of the room. The rest of the lower level is empty. I wonder how many people in this library have read today's newspaper.

I turn my attention to the news story, which details the gruesome history. On March 26, 1980, Marjorie Caldwell visited Helen Hagen at the nursing home in Mound where Helen lived. Alzheimer's disease and diabetes were Helen Hagen's primary diagnoses. Marjorie Caldwell allegedly fed Helen Hagen an unknown food and the next day Helen went into a coma. She died several days later.

The interview with detective Waller flashes in front of me. He told me that the Congdon family and trustees never reported any crime or filed any charges against Marjorie Caldwell after Grandma's suspected overdose of meprobamate because they wanted to avoid the publicity.

My heart is pounding against the thick shell that I have built around it. The staff at the nursing home where Helen Hagen lived and the local police department would not have known about the previous alleged poisoning attempt, as there was no information on record.

I crumple the newspaper and throw it in the wastebasket. The firm ball of bad news makes a loud thud against the metal. I never know when the news stories will appear, where I will read them, or when I will hear the grim details on the broadcast news. I try to stay composed when I see Marjorie Caldwell's picture in the paper or when I hear people talking about her violent history within earshot in a restaurant. It's not the weight on my shoulders; it's the heaviness around my heart.

I try to stand tall even though I'm shrinking inside. There is no one between me, and all the dangers in the world. I am my own bodyguard, my own first responder. But a little voice keeps telling me, "You can do this. You will get through this. Your life is not only this."

I sling my backpack over one shoulder. Then I take a deep breath and put one foot in front of the other, just as Grandma always taught me.

CHAPTER XIV

A PAINFUL INHERITANCE

Not I—not anyone else, can travel that road for you.
You must travel it yourself.
—Walt Whitman

May, 1983

"What is the status of the civil proceedings?" I ask.

"Just let me do my job, Suzanne," the attorney says.

Every time I call the law firm I am pushed away. The behavior of the attorney handling the civil suit has not changed since the first meeting, almost four years ago.

"I'd like to see the billing statements that you've been sending my uncle. I have never received—"

He interrupts me. "I'm trying to work."

"Why is it that I've never been included in any conversations about my own case?"

No answer.

"I would like copies of the statements," I say. "All of them."

I know full well that I will never receive them and I will never be fully informed about the civil proceedings. But somehow, I also know that it's time to withdraw from the case just as I have always planned.

Two days later, the phone rings at my one-bedroom apartment in St. Paul. The attorney's secretary identifies herself and asks me to hold.

A male identifies himself as part of the law firm but he doesn't tell me his name. "Why aren't you continuing with the civil case?" he asks. Clearly, the firm received my letter of intention.

"Who is this?" I ask. "And why isn't my attorney speaking to me?"

"Why are you withdrawing?"

"It's my decision and I would like written acknowledgment of my withdrawal."

"Just tell me why you are withdrawing," the man says. He still hasn't told me his name.

"I've never been treated respectfully, I've never been informed about the progress of the case, and now I'm going to hang up," I say. "I don't want any further calls."

The phone rings nonstop.

I disconnect it from the wall jack.

The next morning I stare at the phone, half expecting it to start ringing. I connect it to the jack, pick up the tan receiver, and dial the number of the law firm. The receptionist answers and I ask to speak to my attorney. I am immediately transferred to the same person who I spoke with the day before.

"Why are you withdrawing," he asks.

"I don't even know who you are," I say. "Either you take my name off the civil suit or I hire someone else to do it."

"I was told to get you back on the case," the man snaps.

"By whom?"

Silence.

"This is my decision," I say firmly.

"You need to be part of the case."

I sense that I am on a speakerphone. I can just imagine a group of suits huddled around a table making hand signals and gestures.

"Please remove my name or I'll hire someone else to do it."

Silence.

"Is that going to be necessary?" I ask.

There's an audible sigh.

"Is it?" I ask.

"No...we'll take care of it."

On July 1, 1983, a settlement is agreed upon and there will be no civil trial. I read about it in the paper although there are no specific details.

But the next day the civil attorney calls. He's abrupt. Doesn't even say hello. "Your siblings have decided that each one of you will give your father a monetary gift in the amount of $17,000 for a total of $119,000."

My stomach is in knots. "I'm not interested," I say. "I have no relationship with him."

"Your siblings have decided," the attorney says gruffly.

"It's my money," I say. "He was never a father to me." I was afraid of the man who hit, who yelled, who walked away, the man who was never a father. I hated him for making my brothers and sisters cry. I don't know about his financial situation but I do know that he was never required to pay child support after the divorce.

"You need to be in my office next week," the attorney says brusquely. "Accountants will be here for the tax-related issues and dispersal of assets. Signatures will be needed."

"I prefer not to be in contact with my siblings," I say. "I'd like to sign the papers privately."

"Everyone will be there," the attorney says. "At the same time." Once again, it's all about control.

"I'd like the details of the settlement," I say. "It was my case and you never included me in the discussions."

Silence.

"I'd like the details," I say. "Now."

The attorney clears his throat. "Your mother will be required to pay all of her outstanding debts, which amount to several million dollars and her attorney fees in the amount of one million dollars. Beyond that she will receive cash and stocks, but a portion of the funds will be held in trust because it's almost certain she will go through the rest of it."

"What trust?" I ask.

"The principal of the newly formed trust will be owned by you and your siblings as part of the settlement agreement. It's completely separate from the money that you will receive outright."

"So we'll never be free of her?" I say. My skin is tingling as if I had rubbed my bare feet against carpet and then touched a wire coat hanger.

"Well, someone has to make sure that your mother will always have something to live on," the civil attorney says. "You and your siblings will own the principal of the trust and you will receive it outright after her death."

"So you've connected us with her indefinitely," I say.

"Well, we thought—"

"You keep saying 'we' but you never tell me a name. Who is it?"

No answer.

Visions of attorneys, bankers, and Marjorie Caldwell Hagen trying to get at this money flash before me. It's true we will never be free of her.

"No one will ever be able to invade that trust. I've taken care of it."

Clearly he has no idea what this woman or her attorneys will do. Maybe he doesn't care. Maybe it's a spiteful decision because I forced a settlement. Marjorie Caldwell Hagen has tried to manipulate trust documents her entire life. The terms of the settlement agreement show clearly that any trust can be challenged in court.

"What about my uncle's remuneration?" I ask.

The attorney quickly changes the subject. "You kids came out extremely well," he says. He details our portion of the settlement agreement and interest in four separate trusts, two of which contain assets that will be distributed outright.

I listen but I barely hear the words. All I can think of is the hideous connection with the criminal who just happens to be my mother and future court hearings with bankers and attorneys who will see this new trust as a free-for-all. I sense the predatory prowess surrounding me. I already feel the sharp talons.

I realize that I will never find out whether the attorney fees included interest or even the actual amount that my uncle was paid back because the documentation is a lump sum, well over $500,000. I don't even know the hourly rate the attorney charged or how many attorneys were actually involved in the case. There has never been any contact from my uncle since the contract was signed other than a dinner meeting with the attorney, one of my sisters, and me. Apparently the arrangements have been a private transaction from the start.

After consulting with yet another attorney, I find out that I don't have to give my father any money. However if I go to court to fight it, the attorney's fees will cost as much or more than the $17,000. I could dispute the entire settlement agreement but my siblings have agreed to the terms and so have the civil attorney and his team, the defense attorney and his associates; even Marjorie Caldwell Hagen agreed after her own drama and efforts to manipulate everyone had ultimately failed. I am the lone holdout. Even though the attorney tries to ignore me I know that my signature is needed for the settlement agreement to be final, as a portion of the assets are legally mine.

"I recommend that you sign the settlement agreement. You are being well-compensated," the consulting attorney says.

I know that the implications of my decision will affect me for the rest of my life.

Complicating things even further is the fact that Roger Caldwell enters into a plea bargain on July 5, 1983. Less than a year before, the Minnesota Supreme Court overturned his convictions on two counts of first-degree murder based on the failed fingerprint evidence.

On September 1, 1982, Roger Caldwell was released from prison pending a new trial. As part of the plea bargain he confessed to the two homicides without implicating anyone else. Astonishingly, before he walks away Roger Caldwell tries to obtain funds from the settlement of the civil case. He petitions the court, somehow thinking that the money signed over to him several days before the homicides by Marjorie Caldwell, her name at the time, is still due. The court denies his request. He isn't entitled to any funds. But a murderer is walking out of prison.

July, 1983

My siblings and their spouses are seated around a long wooden table in the conference room of the law firm. Silently, I take my place in the one empty chair that is left for me. A pile of crisp stock certificates and multiple tax forms are neatly arranged in front of each one of us.

It's so hot in here. I can barely breathe.

One of the accountants from Duluth is standing next to the windows. He looks sympathetic. I almost feel sorry for him, caught in the middle of this mess.

"Each one of the flagged pages needs to be signed," the accountant says as he points to the tax documents.

I do exactly as I'm told but I don't say a word.

"All of you are set for life," the attorney says matter-of-factly. My cheeks flush with embarrassment. The comment makes my stomach turn.

I'm grateful for what he has ended up doing. Even so, I cannot bring myself to thank him. I truly believe that these results were not what he originally intended.

I slide the securities into the large white envelope in front of me and leave the office without acknowledging anyone.

The road curves around Lake Calhoun. Joggers run along the footpath, fishermen toss their lines in search of pike, bass, perch, and sunfish as sailboats tack through the sparkling water.

I crack the window. The lake breeze is mixed with the smell of suntan lotion and wet dogs scampering along the sandy shoreline. The sound of laughter and chatter fills the air, hot dogs and hamburgers sizzle and spit on portable grills.

I glance at the assets on the seat beside me and I wonder how foolish I am to be carrying them around without any form of protection.

Once I reach home, I set the securities on the kitchen table and I drag myself to the navy blue sofa by the window. I flop down, lean my head back, and close my eyes. My head is pounding.

The next morning sun streams through the picture window. I place my hands over the large white envelope. The money that was earned by Great-grandfather Chester and protected by Grandma is now entrusted to me. I feel the energy of each stock certificate as I admire the beautiful artwork, font, and design. The edges are smooth with crisp, pointed corners. I bring each of the certificates to my face and breathe deeply, just a hint of ink. The closely held stock certificates for the family business in oil and gas exploration, mineral rights, and horticultural pursuits have the feel of another place and time. A sense of legacy surrounds me.

In 1892, Great-grandfather Chester moved the family to Duluth, Minnesota, where he joined William W. Billson in a private law practice. There was an air of excitement, because of the discovery of iron ore on the Mesabi Range in northeastern Minnesota.

In the era of men whose names were synonymous with steel, Great-grandfather Chester served as chief counsel for Henry W. Oliver, the Pittsburgh mining executive whose operations on the Mesabi Range produced more iron ore than anyone else's. Chester Congdon protected the interests of the Oliver Iron Mining Company during the merger of the iron mining and steel companies owned by the Scottish steelmaker Andrew Carnegie, the oil king John D. Rockefeller, who quickly entered the iron ore business, the Pittsburgh mining executive Henry Clay Frick, and the head of the largest banking house in the United States and financier for a large part of the steel industry, J. Pierpont Morgan. The merger resulted in the largest corporation in the world, United States Steel.

Great-grandfather learned a great deal about the mining business during the time he was working with Oliver and he subsequently purchased his own ore leases. After Oliver sold the majority of his interest to Carnegie, Oliver shook on an agreement to become partners with Great-grandfather Chester. They each amassed a fortune through mining of iron ore in the Mesabi and Vermillion ranges in Minnesota, and the Gogebic ranges at the far western tip of the upper peninsula of Michigan.

As I glance at the stock certificates I remember the stories Grandma told me about the miners, the men behind the curtain of history. How they moved about the mineshafts, how the candles secured in their cloth caps lighted the way. Carbide lights replaced the candles around 1902 on the Iron Range. It was a measure of progress but an additional risk because the open flame was capable of igniting methane gas in the mines. Years later, I read about the miners and how they faced death from oxygen deprivation, collapsing mines, haulage accidents, and the disturbing prospect of fatal lung disease.

As grateful as I am for the fortune in my hands, I wonder how deserving I am. The challenge is not to take the privilege for granted. I gently touch the stock certificates once again, wondering how I can change a painful inheritance into something positive.

I put my head in my hands and wait, hoping for an answer that doesn't seem to come. After a few minutes I hear a little voice but it's not the one I imagined and it's not the answer to my question. I can't quite make it out so I try to be as quiet as I can and then I hear it again. "I'm here."

The room is quiet and peaceful. It's the voice of Velma Pietila. I just know it. I have always felt unsure as to how I could pay my respects and honor her life because I didn't know what was appropriate or what she would want or even where she is, because she was cremated. No one but her family knows where her remains are located. But I don't question it anymore. It's as if eight years after her death Velma is leading me to a place where she is no longer a victim. She is a heroine.

CHAPTER XV

THE SOUL OF A NIGHTINGALE

I may be compelled to face danger, but never fear it…
— Clara Barton

August, 1983

The white grave markers are arranged symmetrically throughout the hallowed grounds of Arlington National Cemetery. I don't know anyone who is buried here but I immediately feel a spiritual connection. Section 21, the Nurse's Section, is across the road from the Tomb of the Unknown Soldier.

I make my way through the lush green grass, passing more and more white markers until I feel lost in the geometric pattern. I retrace my steps but I can't find the Nurse's Memorial no matter how hard I try. I have to find it. I am desperate to find it.

I stand very still and close my eyes. The sweetness of the freshly mowed grass permeates the air. The leaves rustle in the wind. I slowly open my eyes. I catch my breath. A large granite statue is right ahead of me within a circle of evergreens. It's a moment of grace. As I come closer, the statue of a nurse who represents all nurses stands before me. It's the Nurse's Memorial that I have been searching for.

I gently place my hand within the hand of granite, partially hidden beneath the long cape. It's cool to the touch. I can almost feel the grasp of the fingers.

I look into the face that watches with eternal vigilance over the fallen nightingales buried all around her. I sense Velma Pietila's spirit among them as the rays of sunlight shine through the trees. A cluster of leaves swirls and dances across the emerald lawn like a foliage ballet. The tiny whirlwind sweeps up and down the rows of headstones before heading toward the monument, where the leaves settle. I watch a few rustle, then only one flutters before the wind carries it away.

A red cardinal lands on the right shoulder of the granite statue, flash of crimson. Grandma's spirit is here, too. During World War I she was the state chairman of the Young Women's Safety Auxiliary, a branch of the Minnesota division of the Women's Committee of the Council of National Defense that cooperated with the Naval Service, National Surgical Dressings Committee of the Red Cross, and the American Women's Hospital organization. Grandma worked in cooperation with the chairmen of the Armenian and Assyrian, Belgian, and Polish Relief committees, as well as French Orphan Relief and all the local charities. Along with other women, she completed home nursing and first aid training as part of a reserve force. She rolled bandages, made army packets for the comfort of fighting men, sewed aviators' vests, sold Liberty Bonds, and made Christmas boxes for soldiers and Christmas packages for orphaned children.

The flu pandemic, which began to sweep the world two months before the war's end in 1918, caused even more deaths than the military battles, and the need for nurses multiplied once again. Grandma found a multitude of ways to be of service.

In that era everyone contributed in the best way they knew how. Great-grandfather Chester was elected Vice President of the Red Cross Northland Chapter in 1915, and he donated funds for an improved operating room table at St. Luke's Hospital. Fred Wolvin, Grandma's suitor, volunteered as district manager for membership in the Red Cross. Great-grandmother Clara donated funds to the Syracuse University Nursing program.

As I walk through the neatly mowed grass I think of the public health issues in my own era and the specialty certifications I've earned as a nurse practitioner: Women's Health, Family Practice, and now I also have a strong interest in infectious disease.

The news of a retrovirus as a causative factor of AIDS has spread around the world with at least one case reported in every region. Almost two years ago the AIDS epidemic was the cover story of *Newsweek* magazine. In the first three months of 1983, there were over 150 news stories about the epidemic in major newspapers and magazines and as I walk in Arlington there are over 600. According to figures released by the Centers for Disease Control in August of 1983, there are 2,224 Americans stricken with AIDS and 891 have died. The virus is replicating and spreading, adapting and changing. Its brutality is incalculable and close to home.

It's been almost two months since my friend John died of AIDS-related complications. His partner Matt let me know the news in a letter that I will always keep close to my heart. "John truly hoped for your happiness, a fulfilling nursing career, the love that you so deserve, and the travel and adventures that you yearn for. He decompensated quickly but he was lucid to the end. His ashes were buried next to his beloved grandfather in Kentucky."

Beneath the lush trees of Arlington, I realize that Great-grandfather Chester and Great-grandmother Clara immersed their children in the natural world so they could know it firsthand as a stabilizing force and reservoir of the human spirit. As Grandma found herself and her place in the world, it was still in the wild that she regained a perspective of simplicity and serenity, much like wilderness therapy.

In the midst of the fallen nightingales all around me, it is Africa that is beckoning. The place where I always told Grandma I would go.

CHAPTER XVI

CALL OF THE WILDERNESS

The mountains are calling and I must go.
—John Muir

August, 1985

It's early August, part of the long dry season. Hiking Kilimanjaro is an activity that has wildness, exploration, a bit of danger. The sight of the highest peak in Africa lifts my spirit with a glimpse of the sacred. There is something about looking at this mountain and taking on the adventure and challenge, as well as the blisters and fatigue. It is a mountain that will bring me to my knees by testing my limits and pushing me beyond them much like the mountain of aftershocks since the homicides.

Six months ago, on February 15, 1985, the Minnesota Supreme Court ruled that the trustees and conservators did not have a duty to take measures to guard against the homicides, as their only duty was to protect the house and estate. The justices overturned the lower court ruling and no damages would be paid to the Pietila family, whose wife and mother was brutally killed trying to protect Grandma that fateful night almost eight years before. Justices Wahl and Yetka were the two dissenting voices in the new ruling. I wanted to shake their hands. I wanted to say thank you for trying to bring justice to the Pietila family.

Velma's husband, Loren Pietila, died February 2, 1985. I am grateful that he never learned of the court's reversal.

"My office," Ali says, as he waves his hand toward Kilimanjaro. The head guide has a sparkling smile and generous spirit. Like many of the guides and porters, Ali is a member of the Chagga tribe who have lived and farmed around the base of the sacred mountain for centuries.

"Beautiful," I say, knowing that my dignity over the next week may be left at the base of the mountain itself.

The top of Kilimanjaro is 19,340 feet.

The altitude of the Minneapolis airport is 841 feet.

I try not to think about it. I've done my best to prepare over the past year. I just hope it's enough.

The children have torn clothes and no shoes but they wave and smile as I walk by. Homes with corrugated tin roofs are packed side by side. Rail thin goats traverse the dirt roads. I think of the excess in my own life and I try to bury the shame beneath my lack of self-esteem and the mountain of doubt of who I am.

"Mkipendana mambo huwa sawa. Everything is all right if you love each other," Ali says. He reads one of the Swahili proverbs printed on the material that is used as a skirt, shawl, head wrap, or baby carrier.

A young boy looks at the sky and points. "Jumbo jet," he says. It's Sabena Airlines, the carrier that I had flown from Belgium. The same boy has fashioned a perfect full-sized model of a bicycle from tin and wire. His creativity takes my breath away.

I want to make a difference in the world but I don't know where to start. As I look around me, I already sense that it's the people and the mountain that are making the difference for me.

The next morning I hoist my large olive green duffel onto my shoulder and I make my way to the lobby of the hotel. Two women from Spain, and the accountant from Oregon, are standing beside their own bags. We met yesterday and it's as if we planned to wear matching hiking attire. Tan pants, brown leather boots with multiple scrapes and scuffs, and a rainbow of shirts in green, yellow, red, and blue.

"Jambo," Ali says, as he greets us in Swahili. Trained as a First Responder, he has successfully climbed Kilimanjaro twenty-four times.

Outside the hotel, twelve porters and two assistant guides are patiently waiting. The porters will be carrying all the supplies and gear on their head or back. About fifty pounds each. I am only responsible for my backpack, about fifteen pounds. I already feel like I'm not carrying my weight.

A flaming sunrise of crimson, amber, persimmon, and gold provides a jeweled backdrop during the dusty, jarring five-hour drive to the trailhead. In the distance zebras call out with an occasional high-pitched bark. The exaggerated umbrella-shaped crown of the spiny acacia trees reveals a naturally pruned understory due to extensive browsing by the giraffes.

Each of us describes our training for this momentous undertaking as the dust from the road becomes caked on the windows. "Hiking, running, weight-lifting, and stair-climbing," I say. The others have done much the same. Nervous laughter abounds because we all know there's a certain amount of the unknown as to who will make it to the summit.

The trailhead at 7,300 feet is a welcome sight as we pile out of the truck. We're already more than a mile higher than anything in Minnesota.

As I run my fingers across the leather that is molded to my feet, I notice the patina of soaked-in sweat, dirt, and the wilderness itself. My well-worn hiking boots have been laced up again and again as I trekked through desert, forest, plains, mountains, streams, and windblown areas of the earth: Australia, New Zealand, a polar bear expedition in Churchill, Manitoba, the mountains of France, Great Wall of China, and now Kilimanjaro.

I silently follow the guide and porters along the thick carpet of leaves and moss that blankets the forest floor. African violets and dazzling red impatiens provide exotic beauty along the trail. Tiny rays of sunlight dance among the forest.

The steaming rain forest is covered with bearded lichen, giant ferns, clawing branches, and unruly foliage. Gaiters protect my lower legs and ankles. The red bandana tied loosely around my neck is covered with sweat.

My hiking pole steadies me but it also reminds me of medieval times when walking sticks were used to fight off dogs and wolves. I am fighting the predator of evil and violence with every breath my mother takes and every move she makes.

As darkness descends on the mountain, I lie awake in a small yellow tent that looks like a gumdrop. Unable to sleep, I crawl outside and sit beneath the stars that have oriented wanderers and pilgrims as they navigated their way. I wonder if the incandescence of a single twinkling star amidst a cloak of stardust is Grandma winking back at me.

Each day we move farther upward. The alpine heath is an area of vast openness sprinkled with yellow protea and a flower known as the red-hot poker with its candle-like spikes of red, orange, and yellow. A white-necked raven hovering on the breeze is a constant presence in the moorland zone where there are only tufts of grass and little precipitation.

As we climb higher, layers are essential as there are rapid variations in climate and temperature due to our proximity to the equator and the Indian Ocean. Clearer skies and volcanic rock plateaus, sheer cliffs, lobelia plants like extraterrestrial cactus, and otherworldly giant senecio trees welcome us with their weathered trunks and branches of clustered leaves.

The glint of moonlight on an icy face of the mountain, the ethereal view of a ridge above the mist, and a flash of rose and gold on a distant peak provide glimpses of splendor and transcendent beauty.

The next day I claw my way up Barranco Wall, an 800-foot vertical climb among huge boulders and razor-sharp shards. As I leave a mask of zinc oxide on the natural rock I wonder if anyone in the world would even miss me if I were to fall or succumb to the dangers of high altitude. Acute mountain sickness, high altitude cerebral edema, and high altitude pulmonary edema are often fatal within hours. Altitude is the wild card. The physical challenge, the danger, the wilderness, the dirt and grime, all remind me of the fragile nature of life.

On the seventh day, Ali says, "Twende...let's go!" Zigzagging, moving one foot in front of the other as my boots slip on the gravel and shale, I gasp for breath while the relentless wind slaps my cheeks. The interminable nausea and pounding headache almost overtake me. But I follow the crooked seam that connects me to the guide and others in our group.

We crawl like ants as the natural elements of the wind and clouds swirl around the barren summit. Our faces are ashen from life-threatening levels of oxygen. But we all make it to Uhuru Peak. Wheezing and gasping we stand with our arms around each other, merging with the mountain. The harsh and forbidding environment juxtaposes with the spectacular beauty. "Welcome to God's backyard," Ali says.

Unlike the climb, the descent is knee jarring but much quicker. We literally ski down the loose scree. Once we make it to the stable rock footing, Ali pulls me aside.

"Please help with dreaded disease," he pleads.

I look deeply into his eyes. I see the fear, the threat of HIV and AIDS. Human immunodeficiency virus and the progression to acquired immunodeficiency syndrome are well known on this continent and around the world.

"I take you to kliniki," Ali says. "Meet people."

"I will help," I say.

The next day the members of our group exchange addresses and phone numbers before the others head for Kenya. Ali and I jump into the tan jeep that is waiting and the driver takes off in a cloud of dust as we head to Arusha. Sweat and grime is caked all over my body. My shirt and pants feel crusty against my skin. I am desperate to take a shower but I remind myself that I am fortunate to have clothes, fortunate to be alive.

November, 1992

It's been seven years since I climbed Kilimanjaro, the mountain that showed me I could surmount obstacles in my life by going into the heart of the wilderness. But it was the people who gave me a reason to return to Africa, where I became a part of something much larger than myself. Yet, I still struggle with my own internal wilderness.

The wind howls as I cross-country ski on the snow-covered trail at the Minnesota Landscape Arboretum in Chanhassen. I try to enjoy the beauty of the winter wonderland but just yesterday the newspaper ran yet another story of darkness, violence, and evil. It is true that man has the power to destroy in such a cavalier way and with such brutal disregard that it is beyond comprehension.

On October 29, 1992, Marjorie Caldwell Hagen was convicted of attempted arson for a second time. In 1986 she was released from the women's prison at Shakopee, Minnesota after serving slightly over eight months for arson. This time the fire was in an occupied home. Marjorie Caldwell Hagen requested and was given 24 hours to drive Wally Hagen, her third husband, to Ajo, Arizona, due to his alleged diagnosis of cancer. The following day he was found dead in their home. Suspected cause, asphyxiation by gas. The autopsy showed a toxic quantity of propoxyphene, a prescription barbiturate, but there was no traceable gas in Wally Hagen's system and no evidence of cancer. Marjorie Caldwell Hagen had allegedly waited an extended time before notifying authorities that her husband had died. As a result, the manner of death was undetermined by the coroner. Murder charges were dropped, as suicide could not be ruled out. On October 31, 1992, Marjorie Caldwell Hagen began a fifteen-year sentence for arson at a state prison in Tucson, Arizona.

As I step off the trail and adjust my cross-country ski poles, the faces of individuals, families, and populations struggling with disease and famine and civil unrest flash before me. Every day, men and women from Burma, Somalia, Liberia, Ukraine, Vietnam, Laos, and many other areas of the world pass through the doorway of the clinic in Minneapolis where I am privileged to work. Their diagnoses include hepatitis B, hepatitis C, HIV, tuberculosis, and myriad other health care issues. Many of my patients have been cut off from the roots of their identity. Not just physical immigration or emigration. It's the uprooting of home, a sense of place, and the loss of spiritual and cultural connection.

Like my patients I struggle with who I am and with finding my way back to the heritage I thought was lost, that place where I have not felt worthy or connected since the homicides. When Grandma was killed I didn't know who I was without her and I couldn't find the essential part of myself that fit within the Congdon family and the world.

I'm trying to lead my life in the best way that I can. Even so, there have been many painful arrows of criticism. I know that I can survive the crises in my family but deep inside I know they will not stop. The lethality of Marjorie Caldwell Hagen is unfathomable. She has been associated with four deaths, although there has never been enough evidence to charge her with homicide. I know that she will continue to destroy everything in her path and there's nothing that I can do to stop her.

Several relatives have held out their hands in kindness but I pulled away, having lost my sense of trust. The cruelty by a handful of others has been excruciating. I wanted to tell them all how much I loved Grandma, how hard I tried to be her voice. How my loss is no less than theirs. I wanted to say loudly that I'm nothing like the woman with every characteristic of a psychopath. But I feared they wouldn't listen.

I marvel at the blanketed landscape that extends for miles with icy branches glistening in the sunlight. I reach into my backpack for the scallop shell that I carry with me. It's the same type of shell that Great-grandfather Chester collected and displayed in the curio cabinet in the Little Museum at Glensheen. Grandma let me hold one of the shells in the palm of my hand when I was a little girl. My own shell came with a plain printed card. "There are signs to lead us forward in the midst of a world that is beautiful and broken."

I slide the shell in my fleece-lined pocket and I take off again and blaze a new trail. As I ski through the wooded wonderland I realize that the foundation Grandma built for me was intended to last well beyond her lifetime. Her life blew life into mine. It provided the wind for me to open my wings and soar. She taught me to be kind to others and also to be kind to myself. Grandma shared the family story as part of her legacy and one of her many gifts. It is the richness of her life and the effect of her life on mine that is truly my good fortune. By holding her hand out to me, she taught me to hold mine out to others and they held out their healing hands in return.

I now see that I can choose to join life rather than shrink from it. I can live in the world rather than just live on it. I can always wonder why things weren't any different than they were or I can choose to dedicate myself to making a difference in the world. Having turned to Grandma as I always do, I know that what's next is the path ahead.

PART IV

MESSENGER OF SPRING

CHAPTER XVII

AWAKENING

> Dwell on the beauty of life. Watch the stars, and see
> yourself running with them.
>
> —Marcus Aurelius, *Meditations*

April, 22, 1994

The pale turquoise stationery with my initials embossed in white was a gift from Grandma on my sixteenth birthday. I have saved it for the past 23 years, using it only for special occasions.

I pull out a precious sheet.

With my favorite Mont Blanc pen, a flowery script and a flourish of capital letters, I begin.

Dearest Grandma,

You would have lived an entire century today. I bought one hundred pink wax candles just to see what they would look like on a small white cake decorated with vanilla frosting and yellow-and-purple pansies just like Elna used to make. I lit every candle and it was like a tightly planted pink forest with a canopy of stars.

The portrait that you commissioned of me hangs on my wall. I now see what I had no way of knowing then, the clues within the painting. That little girl's heritage. Her destiny. The power of possibility.

The black velvet of the dress is elegant even though tragedy and loss are deep within its folds. The shadow of darkness whispers to the sunlight. One conceals and the other reveals. The embroidered flowers of the bodice speak to the ravaged wilderness starting to bloom, everything reaching higher for the light.

The unruly cowlick is an emblem of her will to persist, just like the little acorn and oak leaf design of the burnished gold frame. She has a streak of adventure and wanderlust, and Grandma, you made it possible for her to climb mountains, follow penguins and polar bears and elephants, to test her skill and courage, and take it to the limits.

The book in her lap represents education, her eventual nursing career, and her lifelong love of learning.

You knew.

The shoes in the portrait, with the hidden straps, have a story that only you and I know, and the dimple of a hidden smile predicts happiness to come.

The red ribbon intertwined within the bodice, is the red thread of connection between two souls. You have been with me as I completed medical volunteer work in Africa and the beauty of it all was this: when I helped others carry their burdens, I found the strength to carry my own.

I fell in love with a man who cradled tiny babies in his arms and provided volunteer medical care for men, women, and children who fought for life in the slums of Africa. We often worked side by side. He understands and loves the woman that I have become. You would love him, too.

But I struggled, wanting desperately to find the stories of your life. The ones you could not tell after your stroke. I found them, though, in many different places: in Great-grandmother Clara's journals, in archival newspapers, in the Congdon family papers, and in the places where you lived and went to school. I read every word and immersed myself in your history because you are so much more than the last day of your life.

I sent 100 stethoscopes to the Red Cross last week, to be donated to clinics in Africa on your birthday. Usually the nurses don't have a stethoscope of their own but together you and I can change that.

Every day I try to carry myself with a little more grace. I hope that you would be proud. I love you Grandma and I miss you.

November, 1999

There's snow on the ground and the roads are slippery and wet but I make it to the University of Minnesota's St. Paul campus with time to spare. In less than an hour I will defend my doctoral dissertation, *Family Connectedness, Human Relatedness, and Learned Optimism in Late Adolescents.*

My mind wanders back several years to Gothic Thompson Library at Vassar College. A set of five seventeenth-century Belgian tapestries, illustrating the story of Cupid and Psyche, hung on the four interior walls of the great tower.

The librarian pointed to a large stained glass window. "It depicts Elena Lucrezia Cornato Piscopia, the first woman to receive a doctorate, in 1678," she said. "For many years, our students have studied at the table beneath the stained glass window. It brings them luck before exams."

I ran my fingertips along the edge of the table and I pulled out a chair and sat down, just as I pictured Grandma had done more than 80 years before.

"I'm certain she sat here. All the young women did," the librarian said.

I almost skid into the car in front of me but I swerve. I try to keep my mind on the road and for a few minutes I do.

Then I find myself reciting the opening of my research presentation. "Human beings require a context of meaning and hope, a sense of purpose and a larger meaning in life beyond that of routine existence. A deep feeling of being inconsequential to anyone or anything may be experienced as hopelessness, a negative self-concept, and psychological paralysis."

By researching at-risk adolescents, I came to realize that I was studying myself. Grandma fostered safe passage during a dangerous childhood and adolescence with love and connectedness. She cultivated my love of nature and the wilderness, promoted relatedness with others, fostered a love of learning, and nurtured the optimism that is deep within my soul, always tied with a red ribbon to hers. Her love and protection were critical factors that boosted my resistance to potentially harmful, even fatal, situations.

I make it to the St. Paul campus and I park near the veterinary school and clinic. The rustle of hooves and the barking of dogs is close by. The winter air is brisk. Glistening icicles hang from tree branches.

In the pocket of my blue wool dress there's a letter from one of my former patients. The beautiful cream-colored envelope is postmarked December 21, 1990. It was delivered on a snowy Christmas Eve. Inside is a small picture of four little girls in beautiful ruffled party dresses. The letter is in a child's meticulous and careful pencil writing:

Dear Miss Ierroy,
You helped save my life when I was a newborn baby. I am fine now and have no permanent damage. I am nine years old now and I am in the fourth grade. My sisters and I are waiting for Santa Claus to come on Christmas Eve. I want a wheel of fortune game for Christmas, a camera, and a doll. I like to ride horse, help my dad with the cows. I am in 4-H and take piano lessons.
Love, B

She was one of the patients I cared for in 1981, during my first year in Neonatal Intensive Care at the University of Minnesota Hospital. Her diagnosis was congenital diaphragmatic hernia. As a result of the abnormal opening in her diaphragm, some of her abdominal organs appeared in the chest cavity and her lung on the left side did not develop normally.

I thought of her parents and how they helped that little girl know who I am. During that time in my life, they helped me realize that I mattered. My career mattered. What I did with my life mattered.

I am seated at the head of a long wooden table surrounded by five brilliant professors from the schools of Nursing and Family Social Science. Dr. Patricia Tomlinson, Dr. Sheila Corcoran Perry, Dr. Donna Brauer, Dr. Pauline Boss, and Dr. Harold Grotevant.

Dr. Grotevant's lectures in the Family Psychology course made it easier to put the wide-angle lens on what my own family life had been. This kind and intelligent professor told the class, "We must know ourselves before we can help others. Family secrets are harmful."

I remember the statistical methodology class, Latent Variable Structural Equation Modeling. Dr. Geoffrey Maruyama filled six blackboards at lightning speed as I struggled to copy every Greek symbol, number, model, and example; flipping through the pages of my spiral notebook like I was fanning myself. Beads of sweat ran down my spine. It was terrifying, exciting, intriguing, and dangerous because it was so hard. Just like Kilimanjaro and other mountains, I made it because I didn't know I couldn't.

"What have you learned during doctoral education?" the chair of my committee asks. It's the final question.

I think carefully, knowing this is more of a philosophical and personal review. "I will be a lifelong learner," I say. "My education in the classroom and the larger global learning arena, has enriched and broadened my perspective with a lens that gave me the clarity to develop a personal vision of the future. My responsibility is to live my life in a way that makes a difference, just as my grandmother and so many others made a difference for me."

The committee members smile and nod.

I pace the halls as they consider my fate, and then suddenly the door creaks.

I return to my chair at the large rectangular table.

"Congratulations, Dr. LeRoy," they say in unison.

December, 1999

My graduation gown has three black velvet stripes trimmed in gold on each sleeve. The black velour tam has a shiny gold tassel. Inside the tam is one of the two remaining pictures of Grandma and me, slightly faded. The other photo, deteriorating more rapidly, remains in my safety deposit box.

The long gold-and-maroon hood hangs over my arm as I form a line with the other Ph.D. degree recipients from a wide variety of fields.

"Congratulations," another graduate says. A snowy-white feather is attached to the gold tassel on his tam.

"Thank-you," I say. "Congratulations to you, too."

Another graduate has a string of multicolored ribbons, and yet another has a religious medal tied to the tassel. The face of the world is around me.

As we walk into Northrup auditorium, I think of the young girl who didn't know fourth-grade geography and the young woman who subsequently walked it, hiked it, and lived it. I remember how I felt in high school: invisible, a throwaway.

As we ascend the stage, one by one, our names are called.

"Suzanne Congdon LeRoy, Ph.D. in Nursing."

I am not forever bound to the adversity of the past. It's what happened to me, but it isn't who I am or how I'll be defined.

Not any more.

CHAPTER XVIII

LAND OF THE THUNDER DRAGON

Everything in the universe is within you.
—Rumi

April, 2003

As I board Druk Air, the Royal Airline of Bhutan, I turn to admire the hues of fuschia, saffron, and tangerine of the Delhi sunrise. Like the women of India, the sky is dressed in a sari with colors as beautiful as an exotic bird or jeweled butterfly. I'm on my way to the Land of the Thunder Dragon. The beautiful kingdom of Bhutan is thought to exist between heaven and earth, enveloped in happiness.

Fleecy white cloud bundles blanket the sky at high altitude.

I touch the chest pocket of my Land's End jacket and trace the outline of the small leather case that safeguards the deteriorating photos of Grandma and me. It's only a matter of time before the images are completely gone as the old-school Polaroid chemicals continue to degrade.

As the plane slowly descends, the dense cloud bundles become threadlike, resembling white feathers strewn across the sky. There's a mechanical hum as the pilot extends the flaps on the trailing edge of the wings and for a few seconds the plane feels like a glider before it begins a slow and controlled fall.

A few seconds later the plane jolts as the wheels hit the tarmac on one of two airstrips in Paro, the only airport in Bhutan.

As I find my way to the baggage claim, I hear someone say, "Hello, Miss LeRoy."

I turn to look.

A Bhutanese man smiles at me. I glance at his neatly styled short black hair and dark eyes that reflect the rays of the sun streaming through the windows of the small airport. I like him immediately.

"Hello," I say.

"Prem," he says. My guide and Bhutanese chaperone, arranged in advance.

His immaculate striped *gho* is the national dress for men. The cuffed robe is tied at the waist with a narrow woven *kera*. Knee-length black socks and black dress shoes complete his business suit. No trousers.

"Very nice to meet you," I say. "How did you know it was me?"

"Passport photo," he says. "On visa application."

There is a warmth and strength in his handshake. I sense that he's the perfect companion on this very personal journey, leading me on innumerable sacred paths over the next four days.

Prem heads to a bright red Toyota, parked just outside the airport. He slides in the front passenger seat and I get settled in the back.

The driver smiles and nods, and we're off through the beautiful countryside that is so exquisite I think I'm dreaming. I know that forest makes up 70% of Bhutan, comprised of mixed conifers, fir, blue pine, chir pine, and a variety of hardwoods.

"Bhutan is surrounded by China and India," Prem says. He thinks for a minute. "No oceans by you either."

"That's right," I say. "But we have ten thousand lakes in Minnesota."

"Very good," Prem says, as the silent driver negotiates dozens of hairpin turns throughout the steep mountainside and spectacular forest panoramas.

"I have read that Bhutan is a wonderful model for conservation and biodiversity."

"Very good you read about this," Prem says. "National tree is cypress." He switches from his near perfect English and converses briefly with the driver in Dzongkha.

Then he continues for my benefit. "Many plants, flowers, and animals here."

I can almost picture the rhododendrons, magnolias, rare orchids, edelweiss, giant rhubarb, and medicinal plants that are shown in the guidebook.

"Blue poppy, national flower," Prem says. "And at high altitude we have tiger and takin."

"Takin?" I say.

"Takin smaller than yak with short legs, big face, and thick neck. Like moose," he says. "Many other animals, too. Himalayan black bear, leopard, gray langur, goral, red panda, and wild pig."

"Have you seen them all?"

"No," Prem says. "But many. Hundreds of birds live here, too. Many...how you say, maybe no more?"

"Threatened?" I suggest.

Prem nods. "Yes, maybe no more. White-bellied heron, Black-necked crane, imperial eagle, and raven, bird on King's crown."

We pass school children in native dress, young monks in magenta robes, and a group of men practicing archery, a favorite Bhutanese sport.

"Is it possible to buy prayer flags?" I ask.

"Yes, at market," Prem says. "On way to hotel."

"I'd like to take them on our hike tomorrow," I say. "And hang them at Tiger's Nest, the sacred monastery."

"Very spiritual place," Prem says.

I finger the outline of the leather case in my jacket pocket. "My grandmother died twenty-six years ago," I say.

"I believe you are here for special reason," Prem says.

"I had a very special relationship with her." I carefully remove the two photos from the case. "Pictures of us when I was a little girl; but the images are deteriorating."

I place the first photo in the palm of his hand. "This one was taken in my grandmother's garden at the family home." Then I place the second, side-by-side with the first. "And this one was taken at her summer house on a beautiful river where I learned to canoe."

Prem gently touches the edges as he studies each photo.

"Very precious," he says. He carefully hands the photos back to me. "You know about prayer flags?" he asks.

"A little bit. The five colors represent the five elements," I say. "Blue for sky and space, white for air and wind, red for fire, green for water, and yellow for earth."

"Very good, Suzanne. I tell you more. Corners of each flag have pictures of animals: dragon, tiger, snow lion, and garuda, wise bird like eagle. All have special meaning. Wisdom, fearless joy, confidence, gentle power."

I listen carefully.

"Middle of flag is Wind Horse or Lung Ta," Prem says. "Change bad fortune to good fortune. Wind horse carries blessings with speed of wind and strength of horse."

"Where do the blessings go?" I ask.

"Blessings are prayers blown into wind. Spread good wishes and compassion to everyone," Prem says. He thinks for a minute. "We place flags to bring blessings to others."

The driver stops the bright red Toyota near a colorful local market on the side of the road. Richly colored textiles are arranged in neat piles. Sets of cotton prayer flags are rolled up and tied with a white cotton string.

"Around one hundred ngultrum," Prem says. "Under two dollars."

I hand the young man the exact amount, equal in value to the Indian rupee. He picks up a precious bundle and hands it to me.

"I pick you up tomorrow at seven a.m.," Prem says as we arrive at the Gangtey Palace hotel.

"Thank you," I say. "See you tomorrow."

The prayer flags unroll like a beautiful butterfly emerging from a cocoon as I lay them full length on top of the bedspread in my hotel room. The wood block prints have texts and images just as Prem described. Each flag is about twelve inches square with the top edge sewn onto a long thin piece of cream-colored cotton. Extra length, like a ribbon, extends before the first flag and after the fifth flag in order to tie the group to an object.

The case with the photos of Grandma and me is right beside the flags. I didn't know what I would do with the photos once I arrived in this spiritual place but I knew that I wanted them with me and now I have an idea. I take the Brule photo and place it on top of the green flag that represents water. Then I place the other photo, taken at Glensheen, on top of the white flag that represents air and wind. I try to imagine the sky and space where the flags will hang in the sacred mountain region.

My small sewing kit has tightly wound spools of black, blue, and green threads. I strain to see the tiny eye of the needle. It takes several tries to get both dark blue strands through the opening. Then, carefully, I stitch the top edge of each photo to the flag beneath it.

I hold my breath with each tentative stitch. The paper does not tear.

I finish and stand back to admire my work.

Then I fold the five flags, one over the other, careful to avoid bending the precious images before I place them gently in my backpack, leaving the zipper open.

"Goodnight, Grandma," I say.

The next morning Prem meets me in front of the hotel. He's dressed in his beautiful striped *gho* and meticulously polished black shoes.

"Have everything you need?" he asks.

"Yes, precious cargo in my backpack," I say, as I pat the flap.

"We must keep it safe," Prem says.

"Today is my grandmother's birthday, April twenty-second. She would have been a hundred and nine years old," I say.

"Some very old people here in Bhutan. Still work," Prem says. "Cherished for wisdom."

A different driver is behind the wheel but the Bhutanese license plate is the same. We're driven through town on a dirt road in the Paro Valley with no stoplights. Children in traditional dress are on their way to school.

I crack the window. The air smells like the trees of the forest that have lived in this kingdom for years.

The driver parks the car at the beginning of the steep trail surrounded by fertile valleys and broadleaf forests. As I step out, I see people on foot and others riding small horses partway up to Tiger's Nest, Taktsang

Palphug Monastery. Men in traditional dress are holding black umbrellas to shield them from the bright sun.

"You must commit to path like others for over three hundred years," Prem says.

I make my way up the Himalayan path with a man who is, without a doubt, my spiritual teacher. The incredible happiness and contentment that I feel is more profound than I have ever known. By royal decree, Gross National Happiness is more important than Gross National Product in the kingdom of Bhutan.

Through the forest I can see the monastery perched on the side of a cliff 3,000 vertical feet from where we stand. Along the Tibetan border of Bhutan some of the valleys are 11,000 to 28,000 feet where they form part of the Himalayas.

"I like to tell story," Prem says.

I nod.

"There is legend that Guru Ringpoche, precious master, flew from Tibet on back of winged tigress to place we are going. Even took on demon. Precious master stayed in cave. Meditate for three months. He blessed cave, making cave holy. Land became Buddhist nation in eighth century." Prem's face is glowing and serene as he continues the story. "Nine hundred years later, monks climbed mountain to same area. They built temple known as 'Tiger's Nest' around Taktsang Senge Samdup cave. Taktsang means tiger's lair."

Peering through the forest again, I contemplate the monastery that is built right into the rock face on the edge of a precipitous cliff about 10,000 feet above the floor of the Paro Valley. The rock slopes are almost vertical. The cloud cover has lifted over the ethereal site.

"Monastery still here after fire in 1998. Five years ago."

"How did the fire start?" I ask.

"Flickering butter lamps or maybe electrical short circuit," Prem says. "Still working on repairs."

A group of Buddhist monks dressed in magenta robes pass us by as they make their way down the forest-clad mountain path.

A giant prayer wheel is over fifteen feet tall and six feet wide.

"Millions to billions of blessings here," Prem says. "Every time wheel turned, a bell is rung. Blessings spread into world. Carry peace and harmony to everyone."

We walk higher, seemingly to the heavens, as we make our way on the steep switchbacks.

I'm winded in the increasing altitude. I look at Prem. Not a bead of sweat. Not a hint of exertion. His dress shoes are still immaculate.

We pass a teahouse. Then we follow the trail through a grove of moss-covered trees, more prayer wheels, and Buddhist shrines. The stillness is sublime.

I glance at my watch. It's been one and a half hours since we started hiking.

A massive waterfall breaks the silence as a sloping apron drops two hundred feet into a glistening sacred pool. Blue pine trees and prayer flags come into view. The path continues along a cliff that circles the edge of a gorge.

"Seven hundred steps," Prem says. Multiple steps, hand-hewn from stone, first descend then ascend to the monastery. The wood-and-stone façade is a blending of harmony, proportion, and elegance. No nails. No iron bars for support.

We cross a small bridge on our way to the final ascent.

The entryway to the monastery has small temples, brightly colored frescoes, catacombs, and altars. Monks in traditional magenta robes chant sutras. Incense fills the air with the mixed aroma of cardamom, nutmeg, sandalwood, and rose.

Prem kneels and performs a five-point veneration in which the two palms and elbows, two sets of toes and knees, and the forehead are placed on the floor.

I bow my head as he repeats the entire process a total of three times. Then I silently follow him outside.

There's no one around. It's ethereal. Hundreds of prayer flags with frayed edges are dancing in the wind, like mystical birds flapping their wings.

Kneeling beside my rust-colored backpack, I carefully remove the set of folded prayer flags. Brilliant hues are even brighter than I remember.

A strong wind is at my back as I tie one end of the prayer flags to the long string of flags already in place, not far from the monastery. I tug at the knot firmly until it's secure. Then I hold the other end and slowly walk backwards as I watch the flags unfold one by one.

Prem notices the photos. "Very good idea," he whispers.

My fingers move along the edge of each flag. At the opposite end I tie the string to a metal loop and knot it securely.

Then I stand back.

The flags flutter as if they are dancing in unison, happy to be free as they join the others in their message to the universe. The deteriorating images in the photos are suddenly clear again as if I'm back in time experiencing those moments.

It's so quiet. I sense the blessings going into the universe.

Slowly, I pick up my backpack and rejoin Prem. We admire the flags together. Celestial magnificence.

"Prayers of flag become part of universe as they fade," Prem says. "New flags with old are symbol for life changes. Hope for world. Connection among us all."

"Is that true for the photos?" I ask.

"I believe that is true," Prem says.

"Do the mountains sense the blessings...and the images?"

"Mountains speak to each other in many ways," Prem says.

We turn and walk in silence down the beautiful path. Wild white rhododendrons and delicate pink orchids appear to bloom before my eyes.

Two Bhutanese women are near the end of the trail. One is quite elderly but clearly fit and happy to be on the path. I admire her ankle-length *kira,* the traditional dress that consists of a large piece of material draped and fastened over both shoulders with two *koma,* a type of silver hook. The *kera* wrapped around her waist forms a pouch. A bright-pink *wanju,* the blouse that edges the cuffs of her *toego,* is even more brilliant in contrast with the dark blue of her jacket. Immaculately dressed, she walks unaided.

My gaze turns to the young woman beside her dressed in scarlet and emerald green.

"Granddaughter," Prem whispers.

The grandmother smiles and catches my eye.

I smile back.

The cerulean sky is clear.

The mountains whisper to each other in the breeze.

Grandma is as close as my next breath.

EPILOGUE

MISS ELISABETH

Elisabeth Mannering Congdon, the sixth of seven children and third daughter, was likely conceived in July of 1893 during the World's Columbian Exposition in Chicago. The spectacular world's fair commemorated the four-hundredth anniversary of Columbus' discovery of America, and for the first time Congress agreed to authorize and fund a new building that recognized women's contributions to the United States. There were more than 27 million visitors, including Chester and Clara Congdon who visited family in Evanston, Illinois, for three weeks, July 11, 1893 to August 3, 1893.

Nine months later, at 11:00 p.m., April 22, 1894, my grandmother was born at home at 1530 East First Street in Duluth, Minnesota, eleven months after the death of her brother John, two days shy of his second birthday.

The same year, 1894, the novelist Sarah Grand coined the term "New Woman." The New Woman was young, well educated, independent, highly competent, physically strong and fearless, with a strong sense of possibility. The Congdon and Bannister women, from both sides of the family, took Elisabeth under their wings and proudly ushered her into the new era.

In photos, it is my grandmother's demeanor that is distinctive. Her repose as a young girl suggests maturity beyond her years, a collected calm, sturdy determination, and precocious dignity. On February 28, 1898, seven weeks before her fourth birthday, Elisabeth started kindergarten in Duluth, Minnesota, under the direction of Miss Alice Esther Butchart, a teacher of Canadian and English ancestry. Eight months later, on November 1, 1898, Elisabeth was first noted in the Duluth society pages when she attended the birthday party of one of her kindergarten classmates, Miss Margaret Ruth Panton.

My grandmother continued at the University Normal School in Duluth and then she was schooled at home for a short time. On March 20, 1908, her mother Clara documented, "School again—have to set a schedule for E. for her house study. She hates it—says she might as well be in prison."

From 1909 to 1912, Elisabeth completed tenth through twelfth grades at Dana Hall, a private girls' school in Wellesley, Massachusetts. She was elected to membership in Tau Kappa Delta, a council that set the standard for social conduct, and she served along with thirteen other young women during her senior year. On June 9, 1912, the Baccalaureate Service for the graduating class, representing the parting of the ways between school and adult life, included the address, "The Modern American Woman," given by Dr. Robert Speer. He contrasted her with the women of other eras and discussed the enlarged scope of women's activities and opportunities to work for the welfare of humanity. Two days later, on June 11, 1912, the graduation ceremony was held at 5:00 in the afternoon at the Congregational Church in the village of Wellesley, barely eight weeks after the *Titanic* disaster.

Like many young women planning to attend one of the Seven Sisters colleges, Elisabeth took a gap year from 1912 to 1913 to complete extra preparatory coursework prior to taking the entrance exams at Vassar College. She studied Latin and the Roman poet Virgil, complementing her study of Caesar and Cicero at Dana Hall. In September of 1913, at age 19, she entered Vassar College in Poughkeepsie, New York. The rate of American women attending college at that time was approximately five percent. Vassar took women seriously and challenged them intellectually. There were 305 members of the class of 1917, including two international students, one from France, one from Japan, and Edna St. Vincent Millay, a twenty-one-year-old who completed preparatory work at Barnard and would later become a Pulitzer Prize-winning poet.

Elisabeth excelled in solid and spherical geometry, algebra, plane trigonometry, economics, geology, and German. She pursued the cultivation of social reform, women's rights and suffrage, and the prospect of a life of service. However, on September 4, 1915, two weeks before the start of her junior year, Elisabeth withdrew from Vassar.

During the summer of 1915 my grandmother had been evaluated and treated in St. Paul, Minnesota, for health concerns of a gynecological nature, likely dysfunctional bleeding. Clara Congdon documented that Elisabeth's uterus was "displaced" and "must be corrected." In that era, a "displaced uterus" usually meant that it was retroflexed or arched backwards, a cause for concern. Uterine position was determined with a vaginal or recto-vaginal exam and is still evaluated in the same manner today. In modern times however, a retroflexed uterus is considered to be a normal variant.

On June 21, 1915, Elisabeth underwent anesthesia with ether for 43 minutes, during which a uterine curettage and manipulation of the uterine position was performed at a hospital in St. Paul, Minnesota. Pathology was not yet a medical specialty; however, Clara Congdon carefully documented the bacteriologist's findings: uterine fibroids, known to be a non-cancerous muscle and connective tissue tumor commonly associated with heavy bleeding, pain, and infertility.

Multiple post-operative visits, approximately every five days, involved a two-hour train ride each way for an appointment with Dr. Davis or Dr. MacDonald. On July 22, 1915, Clara noted, "E. and I to St. Paul after much tribulation." My grandmother had been very quiet the previous week, staying in bed until late morning every day, which was unusual for her. It's likely that she had been informed that she would have difficulty conceiving in the future. The last documented physician visit for this issue was August 14, 1915.

The Vassar class of 1917 attended during the bulk of World War I, but seventy students (23%) did not complete coursework to receive their diploma. Unlike other students, Elisabeth did not return home to care for a parent. Her father was traveling and overseeing multiple business interests and her mother was involved in the Duluth community, support of foreign missionary work, charitable ventures, entertaining, and travel. Whether my grandmother's decision was related to despondency over recent health issues, concern for the United States' involvement in World War I, or simply the desire to begin new ventures is unknown. However, parents generally provided the most significant influence with these decisions.

Elisabeth kept hidden the things that did not hold her back. Her own Christian principles, instilled by her parents and grandparents on both sides, gave her grace and an inner strength. She accepted her position in society with a sense of duty and obligation, making a difference in her community by disseminating the progressive values she gleaned from her time at Vassar, her mother and sisters, and a long line of women in the Congdon and Bannister families. Elisabeth's paternal great aunt, Mary Satchwell Congdon Hebard, was one of fourteen women arrested in November of 1872, along with Susan B. Anthony, when they voted illegally in New York. Elisabeth worked for women's suffrage and she became a member of the League of Women Voters.

My grandmother's life was full with social activities, membership in the Methodist Episcopal church, and the patriotism of the country as World War I advanced. This not only included efforts to support the soldiers but also to support the animals of war. Along with many other women she participated in a Duluth dog show with her Irish wolfhound, named Wilma, to raise funds for the horses who pulled the carts filled with guns and food and the many dogs that served the soldiers.

In 1919 Elisabeth was elected president of the King's Daughters, an ecumenical group dedicated to silent service. She was re-elected to this role in 1920 and again during the first year of transition to the Junior League of Duluth in 1921.

Over the next ten years she designed a vacation home in Tucson and purchased and completely refurbished a house and additional buildings on the property in Brule. These homes were filled with familiar mementos and her own interior design. No surface of my grandmother's homes was left without a handmade basket, hand-painted pottery, or a simple treasure from her extensive travels. Aesthetics was deeply rooted in her ancestry and her homes became a part of her identity. Throughout her life my grandmother not only maintained her vacation homes but also contributed $50,000 per year for meticulous upkeep of Glensheen, the family estate that is filled with art and artifacts thoughtfully collected by Chester and Clara Congdon.

Elisabeth had an innate ability to mix with everyone and an unaffected enjoyment of the good things in life: homemade strawberry shortcake on the Fourth of July, Indian Pudding, strawberry ice cream that she made in a White Mountain ice cream maker, green grapes with a sour cream and brown sugar sauce, angel food cake, and black licorice. Many desserts were family traditions and she cherished, embraced, and preserved them.

Elisabeth's siblings married for love, joining the Congdon family with other leading families in Duluth and the nation. My grandmother had suitors in Duluth and California, though she declined at least one proposal of marriage. In the United States from 1880 to 1915, the percentage of college women who married ranged from 40% to 65% in comparison to approximately 90% for the general female population. At Vassar, 64% of college students would eventually marry. Although my grandmother chose to remain single, her desire to have a family of her own was never far from her mind.

ADOPTION AND THE
CONGDON FAMILY

Adoption by a single woman was not new to the Congdon family. On September 5, 1892, Clara Congdon noted in her journal that Laura Sophia Congdon, Chester Congdon's 37-year-old-sister, had adopted a two-year-old female named Hope, who had been born in Illinois. Nine years earlier, in 1883, Reverend Martin Van Buren Van Arsdale had organized the Children's Home Society in Illinois. Laura Sophia Congdon married George Hebard on December 31, 1892, and Hope would remain their only child.

Chester and Clara Congdon welcomed Clara's nephew, Alfred Bannister, into their family on April 21, 1898, when he was eight years old. Alfred's mother, Anna Delaval Bannister, died on May 16, 1894, nine days after giving birth to Alfred's little brother, Theodore. In a tragic series of events Alfred's father, Edward Bannister, died on December 13, 1897, and on May 4, 1898, Theodore died several days before his fourth birthday. Alfred became part of the Congdon family, loved and cared for as one of their own, but a formal adoption was never completed. It was Clara and Chester Congdon's desire to have Alfred retain the Bannister name in honor of his father's lineage. Alfred Bannister would later follow in his father's footsteps when he earned a degree from Cornell University.

During the Gilded Age, the advocates of the early adoption agencies included Mrs. Henry Clay Frick, wife of the steel magnate, Margaret Whitney, and the Freylinghuysen and Carnegie families, among others.

In 1922 Mrs. Charles Dana Gibson, wife of the famous artist, and Ruth Chatterton, a New York City actress, promoted the Child Adoption League. By the mid 1920s there had been a gradual breakdown of harsh attitudes toward illegitimacy and professionalism was replacing the voluntarism of the earliest adoption agencies. Mrs. Finley J. Shepard, the former Helen Gould, was a leader among women of wealth who made the "gentle philanthropy" of adoption fashionable and respectable. World War I hero Eddie Rickenbacker adopted two children, followed by New York's "Beau James"—Mayor Jimmie Walker—entertainers George and Gracie Allen, and the "Little Flower" of New York, Fiorello LaGuardia.

Agencies carefully investigated those wanting to adopt, and nine states, including Minnesota, left the responsibility for the investigation to the state welfare departments. The courts were required to notify the departments when a petition for adoption was filed. It was the agency worker who selected a specific child for potential parents based on religion, nationality, compatibility of temperament. In the early 1930s there were approximately 1,500 private institutions in the United States that were authorized to place children for adoption. There were also numerous maternity homes, hospitals, and nurseries such as The Cradle in Illinois, notable for its adoptions to many prominent couples.

There was no precedent for single women of means to adopt; however, through perseverance Elisabeth Congdon adopted a female infant born in Tarboro, North Carolina in 1932, naming her Marjorie Mannering Congdon after her sister and her maternal grandmother. Elisabeth Congdon was 38 years old and the adoption occurred 40 years after her paternal aunt, Laura Sophia Congdon, 37 years old and single at the time, adopted a baby girl in 1892. In 1935 Elisabeth adopted a second female infant who was born in Chicago, Illinois, naming her Jennifer Susan Congdon.

In the early 1930s only five percent of adoptions were formalized through legal procedure; however, Elisabeth Congdon followed proper legal protocol in 1932 and again in 1935.

CONGDON ANCESTRY
AND
FAMILY HISTORY

Elisabeth Congdon's ancestry traces back to England and New England on the paternal Congdon side; and England, New England, and Holland on the maternal Adgate side. Her father, Chester Adgate Congdon, was the son of Reverend Sylvester Laurentus Congdon and Laura Jane Adgate, both from the Hudson River Valley. Chester Congdon's maternal grandmother, Hannah Berger Adgate, was a daughter of the Dutch Van Horne family, partners in the New York banking house of Phillips and Van Horn.

Elisabeth Congdon's mother, Clara Hesperia Bannister, was the daughter of Reverend Edward Bannister, D.D., and Elizabeth Georgiana Mannering Bannister. Reverend Bannister handled educational matters for the Methodist church and was the founder of the private non-sectarian preparatory school, San Jose Academy, and one of 24 trustees and the founding principal of the University of the Pacific, formerly Californian Wesleyan College. A "Female College Institute" was initiated within the university and Elizabeth Bannister became its first preceptress. From 1859-1867, Edward Bannister served as the fourth president of the university.

Clara Hesperia Bannister's ancestry traces back to England on the paternal side and New England on the maternal side. Both the Congdon and Bannister families can be traced to the Mayflower.

CHESTER ADGATE CONGDON
FAMILY TREE

Chester Adgate Congdon   =   Clara Hesperia Bannister
(1853-1916)   (1854-1950)

m. September 9, 1881

Walter Bannister Congdon   (1882-1949)

Edward Chester Congdon   (1885-1940)

Marjorie Congdon   (1887-1971)

Helen Clara Congdon   (1889-1966)

Alfred Edward Bannister (Clara's nephew)   (1890-1952)

John Adgate Congdon   (1891-1893)

ELISABETH MANNERING CONGDON   (1894-1977)

Robert Congdon   (1898-1967)

CHESTER ADGATE CONGDON

Chester Adgate Congdon was born on June 12, 1853, in Rochester, New York. His father, Reverend Sylvester Laurentus Congdon, died shortly after the three youngest children: Walter, Edward, and Helen—all under six years of age—succumbed to scarlet fever. Chester Congdon was fifteen years old when he became the breadwinner for his mother, Laura Jane Adgate Congdon, and two younger siblings, Albert Sylvester Congdon and Laura Sophia Congdon. He would later name three of his own children in memory of his youngest siblings.

Chester Congdon was a member of the first four-year class of Syracuse University, graduating in 1875 with a degree (A.B.) in Classics and additional coursework in Law. He completed additional training, much like a law clerk, with the Syracuse firm of Hiscock, Gifford & Doheny. Chester Congdon passed the bar examination in New York in 1877 and the Minnesota Bar in 1880. He valued his education and continued his relationship with Syracuse University, serving as trustee from 1889 to 1896.

Chester Congdon was appointed United States District Attorney for Minnesota, a position he held from 1881 to 1886. He was twice elected to the Minnesota State Legislature, in 1909 and 1911, and he was elected Republican National Committeeman in 1916.

Through perseverance, vision, and entrepreneurial spirit, Chester Congdon amassed a fortune from mining iron ore in the Mesabi and Vermillion ranges in Minnesota, and the Gogebic ranges at the far western tip of the upper peninsula of Michigan. He was involved in the formation of the Calumet and Arizona Mining Company and successful copper mines were developed at Bisbee and Ajo, Arizona.

Chester Congdon expanded his business interests to include award-winning Aberdeen-Angus cattle and a horticultural enterprise with his own fruit processing and storage warehouse, brand label, and irrigation system. He diversified further with champion Morgan stallion interests, oil and gas exploration, and finance and banking, serving as first vice-president of the American Exchange National Bank in Duluth. He served as director of the Marshall-Wells Hardware Company, the Springfield Glazed Paper Company, the William A. French Furniture Company, and the Gowan-Peyton-Twohy Company.

Chester Congdon played a formative part and significant role in the history of Duluth, including an appointment as one of a fifteen-member commission to prepare a charter for the city. He donated land for Congdon Park and made a gift of funds to purchase thirteen miles of scenic shoreline for a public highway from Lester River to Stony Point, in order to insure the public's permanent access to and enjoyment of the natural beauty and picturesque scenery along the north shore. The highway, completed after his death, was named Congdon Boulevard as a tribute to Chester Congdon and to his wife and children, who saw his vision through to completion.

The family estate, built in 7.6 acres of pristine wilderness on the shores of Lake Superior, honored Chester and Clara Congdon's English ancestry, provided comfort and enjoyment for their family, and a lasting legacy. Chester Congdon would live at Glensheen for eight years until his death on November 21, 1916, in St. Paul, Minnesota. Clara, and four of their children: Walter, Edward, Helen, and Elisabeth were at his side. Chester Adgate Congdon was 63 years old.

CLARA HESPERIA BANNISTER CONGDON

Clara Hesperia Bannister was born on April 29, 1854, in San Francisco, California. She was one of six children and the second of four daughters. Reverend Edward Bannister and Elizabeth Mannering Bannister were determined that all of their children would receive educational advantages. Reverend Bannister often referred to his four daughters as the "Bannister Sorority" and Clara and her sisters, Bertha, Alice, and Mary, all became teachers. Clara's brother Edward became a lawyer, and her brother Alfred became a civil engineer who would later design an irrigation canal in Washington's Yakima Valley for Chester Congdon.

Clara Bannister was one of seven women and thirty-four men in the first four-year class at Syracuse University. Her studies were delayed until November of 1871, three months after her father's death from typhoid fever.

Clara excelled in math and science and she was a talented artist. During her sophomore year at Syracuse University she took an elective course, Acoustics and Optics. Clara had a progressive hearing loss of unknown etiology and would become almost totally deaf by her late twenties. During her junior and senior years she completed four electives: Architectural Drafting, Mechanical Drafting, Art History, and Freehand Drawing. She graduated in 1875 with a Bachelor of Science degree in an era when less than one percent of women attended college. Advanced education was thought to be too stressful for women, a cause of infertility. Clara proved them wrong, later giving birth to seven healthy children.

After graduation in 1875, Clara studied art for several months with Dr. George Fisk Comfort at the College of Fine Arts at Syracuse University. Dr. Comfort, a nineteenth century American scholar and art expert, was one of the founders of the Metropolitan Museum of Art in New York and the Everson Museum of Art in Syracuse.

In 1876 the country was still reeling after the Panic of 1873, but Clara was gainfully employed as Assistant Preceptress of Alexandra College in Belleville, Ontario, from 1876 to 1878. She was unhappy there and subsequently taught art and modern languages at Wyoming Seminary in Kingston, Pennsylvania, from 1878 to 1881, before her marriage to Chester Congdon.

The late nineteenth century was the time during which the infamous Second International Congress on the Education of the Deaf took place in Milan, in 1880. Experts, including Alexander Graham Bell, declared the superiority of oral methods of instruction by the use of speech over those of sign language. Sign language was ultimately banned and thought to be a sign of inferiority. Clara read lips and wrote notes, and family members traced the letters of the alphabet on her hand. Ear trumpets, ear cornets, and Acousticon carbon hearing aids with microphone and earphone were minimally beneficial.

Family portraits depict Clara with a stern demeanor, but that was actually caused by the strain and effort of hearing the conversation around her. She was deeply devout, a biblical scholar, and the moral compass for the family. Like others with deafness, Clara Congdon transformed her life through education in the arts and sciences, her own ways of knowing and appreciating the universe, and her resourcefulness in making connections with her friends, community, and others in the world.

Clara kept meticulous daily notes in a set of journals starting when she was an adolescent and continuing for well over seventy-five years. She noted details about her family, friends, social gatherings, travels, and local, national, and global events. Clara gave lectures, hosted young female missionaries from China, and entertained President Calvin Coolidge and his wife Grace in 1928. The First Lady had completed a training course for teachers at the Clarke School for the Deaf in Massachusetts after graduating from the University of Vermont, which made it easy for the two women to communicate.

Clara Congdon was the last surviving member of the class of 1875 and shortly before her death, she was awarded the George Arents Pioneer Medal for Excellence in Humane and Cultural Pursuits, the highest award Syracuse University can confer on one of its alumnae. She made numerous private donations to Syracuse University throughout her life, the largest of which was in 1928 when she funded the Chester Adgate Congdon Chair in Public Law and Legislation. The chair continues today. Clara Congdon also endowed the chair of the President of the University of the Pacific in 1927, to honor her parents and their dedication to the school. In 1938 she donated additional funds to convert the campus Power House into a library.

Education had long been important to the Bannister and Congdon families. The three oldest Bannister children graduated from the University of the Pacific: Mary Elizabeth Bannister (awarded "Mistress of Science," designated by S.B., 1862), Edward Bannister (A.B.), 1864, and Alfred Bannister (A.B.), 1867. Following the death of Edward Bannister, D.D., his wife and children moved to Syracuse, New York and Syracuse University became a family affair for both the Bannister and Congdon families. Chester Congdon (A.B.) and Clara Bannister (B.S.), both graduated in 1875. Chester's brother, Albert Sylvester Congdon (A.B.), graduated in 1879; his sister, Laura Sophia Congdon (B.P.), graduated in 1881. Two of Clara's sisters graduated from Syracuse University, Mrs. John H. Race (Alice Bannister, B.P., 1881) and Mrs. E.E. Buckman (Bertha M. Bannister, A.B., 1886). Alice Bannister and Laura Sophia Congdon were accomplished artists and studied with Professor George Fisk Comfort just as Clara Bannister Congdon had done. Alice excelled in oils and woodcarving and Laura received the highest praise from the art department for her work in watercolor.

The Phi Beta Kappa chapter at Syracuse University was not started until 1896, 21 years after Chester and Clara graduated. Chester Congdon was elected to receive his key in 1904 and Clara Bannister Congdon was elected to receive hers in 1908.

Chester and Clara Congdon's children received their secondary education from Yale and Vassar, with the exception of Marjorie, who attended Miss May's Finishing School in Italy.

Clara Congdon believed so strongly in education that she offered to pay full tuition for her employees who desired to attend college anywhere in the United States.

Clara Hesperia Bannister Congdon died at Glensheen on July 12, 1950, from progressively increasing congestive heart failure. She was 96 years old and she had lived at Glensheen for 42 years. Clara Congdon was married for 35 years and a widow for almost 34 years. She had outlived her husband, three of her sons, and three of her grandsons.

ELISABETH MANNERING CONGDON PATRONAGES, AWARDS, AND HONORARY DOCTORATES

PATRONAGES

<u>American Red Cross (Northland Chapter)</u>

<u>Arizona Historical Society
(formerly the Arizona Pioneer Historical Society)</u>
The Charles O. Brown house was purchased by Elisabeth Congdon and restored because of her interest in its colorful history as the Congress Hall Saloon, which was built in 1868. It was the town's most popular gaming place and Meeting Hall. In 1961, Elisabeth Congdon donated the Charles O. Brown house to the Arizona Pioneer Historical Society and it is listed on the National Register of Historic Places. Elisabeth Congdon also preserved the Old Adobe Patio, which housed an outdoor restaurant where I ate lunch with her when I was a child.

<u>Courage Center (formerly the Duluth Rehabilitation Center)</u>

<u>Duluth Art Institute (formerly Duluth Art Association)</u>

<u>Duluth Playhouse (formerly the Little Theatre)</u>
Elisabeth Congdon performed in two plays: *Tango Town* and *Overtones*. She entertained the film actress and scriptwriter, Olga Petrova, who was honored with a star on the Hollywood Walk of Fame.

<u>Duluth Yacht Club (formerly Duluth Boat Club)</u>

<u>Duluth Children's Museum (formerly the A.M. Chisholm Museum)</u>
Board Member

<u>Duluth Symphony</u>

<u>Duluth Woman's Club</u> – Head of the House Committee

<u>First Methodist Episcopal Church</u> – member, Sunday school teacher;
Music Committee.

<u>First United Methodist Church</u> – member; supplied and arranged
flowers from the greenhouses at Glensheen.

<u>Goodwill</u> – Director (Duluth, Minnesota)

<u>Junior League of Duluth</u> – elected president in 1921 following the
transition from the King's Daughters; active member of the Junior
League, 1921-1933; honored as Junior League Sustainer of the Year,
November 8, 1961.

<u>King's Daughters</u> – elected president (in 1919 and 1920) of the
ecumenical group devoted to silent service.

<u>Kitchi Gammi Club</u>

<u>League of Women Voters</u>

<u>Lighthouse for the Blind</u>

<u>Matinee Musicale</u>

<u>Minnesota Association for the Physically Handicapped</u>
Board Member

<u>Northern Woman's Home Missionary Society</u>

<u>Northwood Children's Services (formerly Children's Home Society)</u>
Board Member

Northland Country Club

Planned Parenthood Clinic (formerly Duluth Women's Clinic)

Salvation Army

St. Louis County Historical Society – Life Member, 1944

St. Luke's Hospital Volunteer Service Guild
Appointed chairman of nurse's aide training for female volunteers during World War II; rolled bandages, involved in fundraising and war work, just as she did during World War I; Board Member, chairman of the decorating committee (west wing of the hospital and the admittance room); member of the nominating committee; elected Director of the Guild in 1957 and Honorary Director of the Guild in 1967; volunteered in the gift shop and offered her home for annual coffee parties.

Tucson Watercolor Guild

Young Woman's Safety Auxiliary of the Women's Committee of the Council of National Defense
State Chairman (1/19/1918 - 10/1/1918)

EDUCATIONAL PATRONAGES

Dana Hall School – Trustee 1954-1960

Fujian Hwa Nan College (formerly Hwa Nan College)
Foochow, China
Member of American Board

Pine Manor College (formerly Pine Manor Junior College)
One of the founders of Pine Manor Junior College

Syracuse University
Member of Chancellor's Group

Tunghai University (Taiwan)
Donated funds for residence of Dr. The-yao Wu, second president of the University (1958). Awarded Honorary Doctor of Public Service Degree.

University of Pacific
Donated funds for restoration of Bannister Hall. Awarded Honorary Doctor of Public Service Degree on Founders Day, January 6, 1961.

I compiled this list from Elisabeth Congdon's handwritten alumnae records at Vassar College, Clara Bannister Congdon's journals, archival newspapers, and local, national, and global archives.

NOTES AND SOURCES

It was important to me personally and as a researcher, to remedy gaps in my knowledge and verify memories of lived experience to the greatest extent possible. I visited every school, archive, library, and site listed in the bibliography in order to have firsthand access during the research and writing of this book. A multitude of primary materials were consulted: well over a thousand newspaper articles covering more than 125 years, Congdon family papers, personal correspondence, Clara Bannister Congdon's set of journals, and archival records throughout the United States and Europe. Legal documents were reviewed when these were available. Despite exhaustive attempts to obtain the actual transcripts of my testimony during the grand jury hearing and criminal trials, St. Louis County reported they were unable to find the microfilm. Courtroom scenes, testimony, and meetings of a legal nature are recreated from lived experience, personal journal entries, and newspaper accounts.

I have tried to keep citations as concise as possible, quoting only additional facts that I felt would add to the story. The bibliography traces the course of my research for those who would like to delve deeper.

Clara Bannister Congdon's meticulous journal entries are a rich source of information. They provide verification for the stories my grandmother told me as a child and they serve as an outstanding resource for the stories that she could not tell me after her stroke, including: health concerns, surgery and hospitalization, activities, interests, and important events in her life.

Clara Congdon's detailed accounts of her pregnancy with my grandmother are especially enjoyable. By her notes it was easily discerned that conception occurred during a three-week vacation in

Evanston, Illinois, from July 11 to August 3, 1893. During this time frame, Chester and Clara and their family made multiple day trips to the World's Columbian Exposition in Chicago. Clara documented significant symptoms throughout the first six months of her pregnancy, including severe nausea and vomiting, fatigue, leg cramps, heart palpitations, and urinary frequency. Early in her pregnancy she was unable to keep anything down except for soup or clam bouillon. Clara Congdon was a tiny woman and at 13 weeks gestation (just over three months into her pregnancy) she weighed only 102 pounds. She walked almost daily, often with my great-grandfather, as many as 30 blocks in one day. In a humorous light, she described the need to frequently relieve herself in "the corner," the location of the ladies' restroom at the Spaulding Hotel in downtown Duluth. After the first six months of her pregnancy Clara was feeling much better and her journal entries concentrated on the details of her family and daily activities until my grandmother's birth on April 22, 1894.

The society pages of the Duluth newspaper provided vivid descriptions of my grandmother's evening gowns and accessories and the wide array of social and charitable events that she hosted or attended beginning when she was a young girl and continuing throughout her life. Reading the detailed accounts, not all of which are noted in this book, I could almost hear the rustle of silk, smell the aroma of sweet peas and nasturtiums, feel the tight white gloves buttoned to the elbow, and envision the details of my grandmother's delicate jade fan.

SELECTED BIBLIOGRAPHY

ARCHIVES AND COLLECTIONS

American Red Cross Archives, Washington, D.C.

First United Methodist Church Archives, Duluth, Minnesota

Glensheen Archives, University of Minnesota-Duluth

Holt-Atherton Special Collections, University of Pacific Library, Stockton, California

Lloyd's Register of Ships

Lloyd's Register of Yachts

Nina Heald Weber Archives 1949, Helen Temple Cooks Library, Dana Hall School, Wellesley, Massachusetts

Northeast Minnesota Historical Center, Duluth, Minnesota

Phi Beta Kappa, Kappa Chapter of New York at Syracuse University

Special Collections, Thomson Library, Vassar College, Poughkeepsie, New York

Special Collections Research Center, Syracuse University Library, Syracuse, New York

St. Louis County Historical Society Archives, Duluth, Minnesota

University of Arizona Special Collections Library, Tucson, Arizona

U.S. National Archives and Records Administration, Washington, D.C.

MANUSCRIPT COLLECTIONS

Chester Adgate Congdon Papers, Glensheen, Duluth, Minnesota

Clara Bannister Congdon Journals, Glensheen, Duluth, Minnesota

Elisabeth Mannering Congdon Papers, Swiftwater Farm, Brule, WI

NEWSPAPERS

Extensive review of newspapers included more than 1,000 articles researching the Congdon family history. From 1977 to 2012, the majority of articles are related to the criminal and civil proceedings.

Arizona Daily Star, Tucson, Arizona
Bay City Times, Bay City, Michigan
Brainerd Daily Dispatch, Brainerd, Minnesota
Corning Daily Journal, Corning, New York
Daily Olympian, Olympia, New York
Duluth News-Tribune, Duluth, Minnesota (1881-2012)
Duluth Evening Herald, Duluth, Minnesota
Hastings Star Gazette, Hastings, Minnesota
Minneapolis Star-Tribune, Minneapolis, Minnesota
Morning Olympian, Olympia, Washington
Northern Christian Advocate, Syracuse, New York
Phoenix Gazette, Phoenix, Arizona
San Jose Mercury News, San Jose, Califonia
Seattle Daily Times, Seattle, Washington
St. Paul Pioneer Press, St. Paul, Minnesota
The Patriot-News, Harrisburg, Pennsylvania
Tucson Citizen, Tucson, Arizona

BOOKS

Chesler, Ellen. *Woman of Valor: Margaret Sanger and the birth control movement in America.* New York: Simon & Schuster, 1992.

Cochran, Michael J. *Invincible: History of the Duluth boat club, established 1886.* Duluth, MN: The Donning Company, 2008.

Cooper, Wyatt. *Families: A memoir and a celebration.* New York: Harper & Row, 1971.

Delano, Jane A., and Isabel McIsaac. *American Red Cross Textbook on Home Hygiene and Care of the Sick.* Philadelphia: P. Blakiston's Son & Co.,1913.

Flexner, Eleanor, and Ellen Fitzpatrick. *Century of Struggle: The woman's rights movement in the United States.* Cambridge: The Belknap Press of Harvard University Press, 1996.

Fourie, Ada. *Their Roots Run Deep.* Duluth, MN: University of Minnesota (not dated).

Gibson, Elizabeth. *Images of America: Yakima, Washington.* Charleston, SC: Arcadia Publishing, 2002.

Hirsch, Edward, ed. *To a Nightingale: Sonnets and poems from Sappho to Borges.* New York: George Braziller, Inc., 2007.

Hoover, Roy. O. *A Lake Superior Lawyer: A biography of Chester Adgate Congdon.* Duluth, MN: Superior Partners, Ltd., 1997.

Johnson, John M. *Southern Women at the Seven Sisters Colleges: Feminist values and social activism 1875-1915.* Athens: The University of Georgia Press, 2008.

Lane, Michael. *Glensheen: The construction years.* Duluth, MN: Glensheen, Property of the University of Minnesota, (not dated).

Lang, Harry G., and Bonnie Meath-Lang. *Deaf Persons in the Arts and Sciences: A biographical dictionary.* Westport, CT: Greenwood Press, 1995.

Matthews, Jean V. *The Rise of the New Woman: The women's movement in America, 1875-1930.* Chicago: Ivan R. Dee, 2003.

Milford, Nancy. *Savage Beauty: The life of Edna St. Vincent Millay.* New York: Random House, 2001.

Miller, Donald L. *City of the Century: The epic of Chicago and the making of America.* New York: Simon & Schuster, 1997.

Norton, Maryanne C., and Sheldon T. Aubut. *Images of America: Duluth, Minnesota.* Charleston, SC: Arcadia Publishing, (not dated).

Patterson, Martha H., ed. *The American New Woman Revisited: A reader, 1894-1930.* New Brunswick: Rutgers University Press, 2008.

Sanger, Margaret. *The Autobiography of Margaret Sanger.* Minneola, NY: Dover Publications: 2004.

Schilts, Randy. *And the Band Played On: Politics, people, and the AIDS epidemic, 20th anniversary edition.* New York: St. Martins, 1987, 1988.

Scott, Anne F. *Natural Allies: Women's associations in American history.* Urbana: University of Illinois Press, 1992.

Soetebier, Virginia M. *Footnote to History.* Duluth, MN: Stewart-Taylor Printing, 1995.

Sunderland, Jabez Thomas. *The Door of New Opportunity Open to Educate Young Women: A sermon preached to the King's Daughters.* Ann Arbor, MI: Ann Arbor Publishing, 1891. Historical Reproduction by BiblioLife, LLC, (not dated).

University of Minnesota School of Fine Arts. *Glensheen.* Duluth, MN, (not dated).

Woosley, Anne I., and the Arizona Historical Society. *Images of America: Early Tucson.* Charleston, SC: Arcadia Publishing, 2008.

Zimmerman, Jean. *Love, Fiercely: A gilded age romance.* New York: Houghton Mifflin Harcourt, 2012.

ARTICLES

Gringeri-Brown, Michelle. "Glensheen: A Craftsman Country Estate," *American Bungalow,* 23, (Fall, 1999), 14-20.

Webb, Jennifer D. "Golden Age Collecting in America's Middle West: Chester and Clara Congdon's Glensheen Historical Manor and Raymond Wyer's *An Art Museum," Journal of the History of Collections (Advance Access Publication),* 22, no.1, (August 14, 2009), 99-113.

DOCTORAL DISSERTATIONS

LeRoy, Suzanne Congdon. Family Connectedness, Human Relatedness, and Learned Optimism in Late Adolescents. (1999) Ph.D. Dissertation, University of Minnesota.

Romanofsky, Peter. The History of Adoption Practices, 1870-1930. (1969) Ph.D. Dissertation, University of Missouri.

FILM

You'll Like My Mother. Dir. Lamont Johnson. Perf. Patty Duke, Rosemary Murphy, Richard Thomas, Sian Barbara Allan. Bing Crosby Productions, Universal Studios (1972). Motion Picture.

ACKNOWLEDGMENTS

This book would not be what it is without the many individuals who helped bring it to life. My editor, Bill Roorbach, took me on as a fledgling as I struggled to face the page. His patience, kindness, and loyalty have been steadfast, even in the midst of his own literary endeavors.

Scott Edelstein read the manuscript, offered valuable insight, thought-provoking discussion, and gracious assistance.

Multiple archivists and librarians supported my research efforts. Pam Kaplan, Nina Heald 1949 Archives, Dana Hall School, spent an entire day sharing records, photos, and scrapbooks from my grandmother's era. I am deeply grateful for her generous and gracious support. Dean Rogers, Special Collections Assistant, Vassar College Library, patiently answered my questions and arranged for student handbooks, papers, and countless resources in the Vassar archives. Michael Wurtz, Holt-Atherton Special Collections, University of the Pacific Library, has been an invaluable and conscientious resource. Dr. Philip Gilbertson, Provost of the University of the Pacific (1996-2010) generously shared his research and insight regarding my great-great-grandfather, Edward Bannister, one of the founders and the fourth president of the school. Mary O'Brien, Special Collections Research and University Archives, Syracuse University, kindly provided access to original documents and letters related to the Congdon family and countless other resources. Patricia Maus, Curator, Special Collections, Northeast Minnesota Historical Center, graciously shared her expertise and provided access to multiple resources. Fujian Hwa Nan Women's College, Foreign Affairs Office, very cordially responded to my request for information. My thanks to Linda Rau, Reference Librarian, Duluth Public Library, for her kindness and invaluable assistance. Mary Matlack, Director Volunteer

Services, St. Luke's Hospital, Duluth, MN, personally wrote me a wonderful letter about my grandmother's volunteer work.

Whitney Hopkins, American Red Cross, Washington, D.C., arranged an outstanding private tour and detailed explanation of the Red Cross history.

Anne Cowne, Information officer, Lloyd's Register Group Services, Ltd., London, UK, generously shared her time, patience, and expertise researching information about the *Hesperia* yacht and the *Chester A. Congdon*.

Commodore Mike Contris and Lisa Mighetto, Olympia Yacht Club, provided wonderful assistance as I delved into the history of the *Sea Wolf.*

Guy Kawasaki, Carla King, Joel Friedlander, and Dan Poynter continue to provide the highest quality books, workshops, online resources, and mentorship to the writing community. Their contributions to self-publishing have opened the doors.

The San Francisco Writer's Conference, under the expert direction of Elizabeth Pomada and Michael Larsen, has been an extraordinary resource over the past three years.

Special thanks to Eve Ness for copy-editing, enthusiasm, and wonderful support as the book came to fruition.

Steve Bye's expertise with the archival photos from my personal collection has been invaluable. His passion for photography and a quality outcome is truly extraordinary.

Pamela Harden, my closest friend for almost forty years, has supported me from the beginning. Thank you for always believing in me, standing beside me, and walking with me. Thank you to Chris Harden, Pam's husband, and Bernice King, Pam's mother, for always making me feel like part of the family. And to Rupert, their wonderful Scottish terrier, thank you for making me laugh.

My heartfelt thanks to the nursing colleagues who wrapped their capes around me when I needed it most: Dixie Anderson, Candace Birk, Karen Brand, Ellen Egan, Barbara Hoglund, Kathy Huntington, Beverly Rutledge, Neda Tasson, and the nursing faculty who were part of my doctoral committee at the University of Minnesota: Dr. Patricia Tomlinson, Dr. Sheila Corcoran-Perry, and Dr. Donna Brauer. Dr. Patricia Crisham, you were always on my committee in spirit.

To my doctoral committee members in Family Social Science: Dr. Pauline Boss and Dr. Harold Grotevant (currently Rudd Family Foundation Chair in Psychology, University of Massachusetts-Amherst). Thank you for graciously showing me the way.

Posthumously, my heartfelt gratitude to the following individuals who helped me reach for the light during difficult times: Anna Bergman, Ida Bowman, Helen Congdon d'Autremont, Marjorie Congdon Dudley and Harry Chittenden Dudley, Persis Browne Congdon, Stephen House Congdon, Carl and Elna Pearson, Zandra Powers, Ida Ramsey, James and Sarah Roper, Hans Senn, and Clara Congdon Spencer.

To those many others who have silently supported me during difficult times, I have felt your presence.

I deeply thank you all.

AUTHOR'S NOTE

All events in this book are true. There are no composite characters or events. No names have been changed, although some individuals are identified only by first name, or in several instances by occupation or family relation due to privacy and security concerns. Reconstructed dialogue is based on memory and my personal notes and journals; it is of course impossible to recreate exact word-for-word discussions. There were no interviews. Members of my immediate and extended family, and those involved in the criminal and civil cases, may have different memories.

On January 5, 2004, Marjorie Caldwell Hagen was released from the Arizona State Women's Prison after serving eleven years, two months, and four days of a fifteen-year sentence for arson. It was her second incarceration for arson.

On March 1, 2007, Roger Sammis, an elderly man with a cardiac condition, died in a Tucson, Arizona, hospital. He had signed over power of attorney to Marjorie Hagen and his body was cremated immediately. On March 22, 2007, Marjorie Caldwell Hagen was arrested and charged with fraud, computer tampering, forgery, and theft of an $11,181.04 check that Roger Sammis had received as an inheritance. With no body and no autopsy, she could not be charged with murder. After multiple delays in the legal process, Marjorie Caldwell Hagen pleaded guilty to attempted forgery on November 17, 2008. On March 4, 2009, she was sentenced to three years intensive probation as part of a plea agreement.

ABOUT THE AUTHOR

Suzanne Congdon LeRoy has been a nurse practitioner for 30 years with specialty certifications in Women's Health, Family Practice, and advanced practice HIV/AIDS. She completed her Bachelors, Masters, and Ph.D. in Nursing at the University of Minnesota, post-graduate training at Planned Parenthood and Metropolitan State University, and executive education at the University of St. Thomas and Harvard Kennedy School. She is a member of the Junior League of Minneapolis, the Woman's Club of Minneapolis, and a Northside Achievement Zone Friend of the Future.

Nightingale is her first book. A portion of the proceeds will be used to support health and human rights initiatives that benefit women and girls with an emphasis on education, reproductive health, and violence prevention.

www.SuzanneCongdonLeRoy.com

CPSIA information can be obtained at www.ICGtesting.com
Printed in the USA
LVOW11s1603150914

404140LV00002B/290/P